THE WHITE PRESS
AND
BLACK AMERICA

The White Press
and
Black America

CAROLYN MARTINDALE

CONTRIBUTIONS IN AFRO-AMERICAN
AND AFRICAN STUDIES, NUMBER 97

GREENWOOD PRESS
NEW YORK • WESTPORT, CONNECTICUT • LONDON

Burgess
PN
4882.5
.M38
1986
COPY 1

Library of Congress Cataloging-in-Publication Data

Martindale, Carolyn, 1938–
   The white press and Black America.

   (Contributions in Afro-American and African studies,
ISSN 0069-9624 ; no. 97)
    Bibliography: p.
    Includes index.
    1. Afro-Americans in the press. 2. American
newspapers. 3. Race relations and the press—United
States. I. Title. II. Series.
PN4882.5.M38   1986   071'.3'08996   85-27219
ISBN 0-313-25103-7 (lib. bdg. : alk. paper)

Library of Congress Catalog Card Number: 85-27219
ISBN: 0-313-25103-7
ISSN: 0069-9624

First published in 1986

Greenwood Press, Inc.
88 Post Road West, Westport, Connecticut 06881

Printed in the United States of America

The paper used in this book complies with the
Permanent Paper Standard issued by the National
Information Standards Organization (Z39.48-1984).

10 9 8 7 6 5 4 3 2 1

Contents

viii Contents

List of Illustrations

List of Tables

THE WHITE PRESS
AND
BLACK AMERICA

CHAPTER 1

Why Study Racial Coverage?

Equality and justice are long-enshrined ideals of American society, but they have never been a reality for millions of black Americans. Although important strides toward achieving these goals were made during the civil rights revolution of the 1960s, racial discrimination continues to constrict the lives of many black Americans and to deprive white Americans of the opportunity to relate to a large number of their fellow citizens. The mass communications media, whether they desire the role or not, play a vital part in this situation.

Most American journalists, no matter how committed personally to ideals of equality, would shy away from the suggestion that the media should deliberately undertake the task of trying to improve race relations. Such an idea seems to imply managing the news—a practice completely contrary to the journalist's obligation to "tell it like it is."

However, the way the media portray black Americans and report on relations between the races strongly influences the way the public perceives these aspects of American life. Media reportage can promote attitudes of acceptance, or of hostility and fear; it can increase understanding, or it can encourage repression; it can expose problems and present suggested solutions, or it can ignore uncomfortable situations until they explode into violence.

One fact the upheavals of the 1960s made clear to many reporters was that following traditional journalistic practices in covering the race story was as likely as not to produce one of the negative effects mentioned above. Because of the story's complexity and sensitivity, and because of decades of journalistic and public inattention to the situation of black Americans, simply "telling it like it is" in news coverage often reinforced the very attitudes the media were decrying in editorials. Journalists came to recognize some of the deficiencies of their coverage and began seeking ways to improve it.

During the decade following the U.S. Supreme Court's school desegregation decision in 1954, the tempo of American blacks' long struggle for equality increased dramatically. Boycotts and sit-ins and freedom rides focused attention on segregation of transportation and other public facilities, violence met federally enforced school desegregation and attempts to secure voting rights in many parts of the South, and several major civil rights acts were passed. Then, disorders began flaring up in the black sections of cities in the North and West.

By the middle of the decade it was clear that the nation was experiencing a serious racial crisis, and journalists began to devote increasing attention, in conferences and professional periodicals, to the nature of their coverage of America's racial situation. In 1965, members of the press from throughout the country discussed "The Racial Crisis and the News Media" at a conference at the University of Missouri's School of Journalism. In 1967, a symposium on "The Black American and the Press" was sponsored by the UCLA Foreign Journalism Awards program and another conference on mass media and race relations was conducted by the American Jewish Committee at Columbia University Graduate School of Journalism for the Community Relations Service of the U.S. Justice Department.

The period in which these meetings were held also saw increasing white resistance to integration throughout the country, ghetto riots in hundreds of cities, the assassination of Dr. Martin Luther King, Jr., and anti-segregation actions by various branches of the federal government. In 1968 the National Advisory Commission on Civil Disorders, appointed by President Johnson to investigate the causes of the ghetto riots, issued its report. In its section on the media, the report echoed many of the concerns already expressed by journalists about the nature of media coverage of black Americans and the nation's racial crisis.

In May of 1968 the University of Chicago Center for Policy Study held a conference to discuss the media-related issues raised by the National Advisory Commission, also known as the Kerner Commission. The commission's chapter on the media also was used as a resource for journalists and black citizens from Washington and Oregon participating in a June 1968 symposium on "The Newsman and the Race Story" held at the University of Washington in cooperation with the U.S. Justice Department's Community Relations Service.

The major findings of the commission were that the media had made a substantial effort to present a balanced and factual account of the disorders but had nonetheless exaggerated both the mood and scale of the disturbances. Even more important, the commission said, the media had failed to report adequately on the causes underlying the disorders and problems in race relations. The commission added that the media had failed to convey to their white audiences what it was like to be black in America.[1]

One of the common themes running through the discussions of coverage of racial matters by media representatives and members of the Kerner Commission was the idea that it is the media's responsibility to keep the public informed of injustices and other social maladies that may flare into violence. In his introduction to the report on the UCLA conference, Jack Lyle, referring to the Watts riots, asked: "Are not the institutionalized information media seriously failing if they do not alert us to festering conditions so that they may be treated before they erupt and infect the entire society?" How can citizens be expected to be concerned and bring pressure to correct the inequalities within a society, he asked, "if the agencies to whom they have delegated responsibility for maintaining the societal surveillance do not sound the alarm?"[2]

A similar observation was made by Lawrence Schneider in his introduction to the University of Washington seminar report. Remarking upon journalists' ignorance of black America, he wrote: "Although charged with the responsibility of keeping a close check on government, of rooting out injustice and of protecting the weak, the American press . . . had not discovered the problems of the Black man in America, nor had it led in the struggle to solve the problems."[3]

This view, which also was expressed by participants in the other seminars, was echoed by the Kerner Commission, which stated its opinion that "it is the responsibility of the news media to tell the story of race relations in America."[4]

Ben Gilbert, a *Washington Post* editor, discussed the subject in an article in the *ASNE* (American Society of Newspaper Editors) *Bulletin* after the Kerner report was released. He said he felt most newspaper editors would agree with the commission's claim that it was the news media's responsibility to keep Americans informed of the nation's racial situation.[5]

A few months later, in its special section on the Kerner report, the *Columbia Journalism Review* reported on a survey it had made of nearly 400 executives of American newspapers, magazines, and radio and television stations. The executives said they felt the media's role should be to inform and educate the public about racial problems.[6]

Whether or not it is indeed the media's responsibility to tell the story of race relations in America, and what kinds of coverage would fulfill that responsibility, will be discussed more fully in the next chapter. The point to be made here, however, is that during the second half of the 1960s many media professionals, as well as observers, seemed to believe that the media had such a responsibility.

Since that time the confrontational events of the civil rights struggle have dwindled, and media attention has been captured by the war in Viet Nam, Watergate, and a host of other concerns. Because many civil rights gains were made by blacks during the 1960s, and because sit-ins and anti-integration violence and riots have seldom occurred and caught media attention in the past decade, many white Americans seem to believe that the nation's racial problems have been largely overcome.

As Lyle observed, the event-orientation of American journalism has conditioned readers to perceive the news as a succession of crises which are thrust upon their attention and then disappear; "the citizen-reader assumes that the crises have been successfully resolved as they no longer appear in the media."[7]

But the problems that precipitated the crises of the civil rights struggle of the 1960s and the ghetto riots have not disappeared, although some of them have been alleviated. In fact, it can be argued that for many—perhaps most—American blacks not much has changed since 1968, when the Kerner report sketched a stark picture of the American black's position at the bottom of society's socioeconomic ladder.

SITUATION OF BLACK AMERICANS

A few examples will suggest the dimensions of the problem. The following data illustrate clearly how few real gains were made during the decade of the 1970s against continued discrimination in employment and housing, inadequate schools and health care, the erosion of family structure among many low-income blacks, and inequality before the law.

The 1980 census indicated that 26.4 million Americans, or 11.7 percent of the nation's population, were black. At that time 56 percent of the black population still lived in the high-crime and poverty-ridden ghettos of the nation's cities.[8]

In 1969 the median family income of blacks was 61 percent that of whites, but because of inflation and the general slowdown of the national economy, by 1980 the ratio was down to 59 percent.[9]

In 1966 the percentage of the black population living in poverty was 42 percent, compared to 11 percent of whites. In 1979, 31 percent of the nation's blacks, compared to 9 percent of the whites, were living in poverty.[10]

In 1966 unemployment among nonwhites was 7.3 percent, compared to 3.3 percent for whites. In November of 1982 unemployment among black males was 19 percent, compared to 9.2 percent for white males. Even in 1980, before the recession deepened, the unemployment rate for black college graduates was the same as the rate for white high school dropouts, and it was almost twice that of whites who never went to college.[11]

In 1965 the proportion of black families headed by women was 24 percent, compared to 9 percent among whites. By 1980, 44 percent of all black children were living with only one parent.[12]

In 1980 blacks comprised 53.5 percent of the nation's prison population.[13]

In 1973 life expectancy for blacks was still about six years less than that of whites, while in 1978 infant mortality rates among children from one month to one year old were twice as high among blacks and other nonwhites as among whites.[14]

These data reveal only part of the picture. Despite the legislative civil rights gains achieved during the 1960s, the increased participation of black voters and black leaders in the political process, and the advances of black professional persons, many black Americans share a perception that their situation is not better and, indeed, is getting worse.

In 1981 reporters for the Gannett News Service conducted over 200 interviews with black citizens in 45 cities and towns in 14 states. "Underlying virtually all the interviews," their report stated, "was a pervasive feeling that racism is so deeply a part of American life that it undermines all efforts to make equality a reality."

According to the report, the Kerner Commission's prediction that "our nation is moving toward two societies, one black, one white—separate and unequal" describes for many black Americans the United States as it is today. The report also quotes the U.S. Civil Rights Commission's urgent message to the president and congressional leaders early in 1981 expressing the commission's concern over "increased resistance to civil rights progress, the resurfacing of hate groups, the growing frustration of millions of Americans for whom promises remain unfulfilled."[15]

These observations echo the findings of a ten-part series on blacks in America published by the *Wall Street Journal* in 1980. The *Journal's* reporters also found that in many fields blacks' progress was more statistical than real and that racism remained a powerful barrier to equality in employment, housing, and education.[16]

If the conditions that led to the ghetto riots of the 1960s persist largely unresolved today, and racism remains a powerful obstruction to black equality, are the media attempting to inform the public of this situation? If they are, is the coverage provided adequate to convey to whites, as the Kerner Commission urged it should, "a feeling for the difficulties and frustrations of being a Negro in the United States"? Does it also present, as the commission suggested, "a sense of the degradation, misery and helplessness of living in the ghetto"?[17] An attempt to find some answers to these questions underlies the coverage study reported in this book.

Besides failing to convey to whites a sense of the reality of being black in America, the media also had not portrayed the contributions of blacks to American society, the Kerner Commission said. "They have not shown understanding or appreciation of—and thus have not communicated—a sense of Negro culture, thought, or history," stated the commission.[18]

It seems noteworthy that although blacks represent only 12 percent of the nation's population, and have 31 percent of its poverty, they also have produced outstanding men and women far out of proportion to their numbers. Blacks comprise a very large percentage of America's finest athletes and musicians—two professions traditionally not closed to blacks—and, more recently, have assumed political leadership of many of the nation's largest cities and in Congress and state and local government.

In addition, American blacks have made significant contributions in literature, to the development of various forms of music in this country, and in other fields of endeavor. They have produced great men and women such as W. E. B. DuBois, Frederick Douglass, Harriet Tubman, and Martin Luther King, Jr. It seems ironic that many white people regard Martin Luther King Day as a holiday set aside to honor a black hero, when in actuality Dr. King also was an *American* hero whom Americans of any race can be proud to claim.

It also seems ironic that the African heritage brought to this country by black slaves and woven into America's culture should be so overlooked. Much is made in our national life of this nation's ties with European countries, through the many immigrants who thronged to the New World. But surely America has ties just as real, and even older, with the west coast of Africa. Enslaved Africans were brought to this country over a century before the first waves of European immigrants arrived and in numbers that must rival the immigration from some European countries. Yet because much of this heritage has been lost, and perhaps because white Americans are reluctant to acknowledge it, the African strains in American culture have gone unremarked in the media and elsewhere, while the contributions of other nations' cultures have been heralded.

Obviously, covering the experience of the black American adequately would involve coverage of strengths as well as problems. It might involve, for instance, covering the establishment of a black grocery store cooperative in an urban neighborhood as well as portraying the plight of an inner-city black child trapped in an inadequate school. Better coverage of black Americans also would mean covering black contributions and interesting individuals as well as examining the oppression which many blacks experience. Readers should be exposed not only to stories about inequalities in the administration of justice, for example, but also to pieces on the achievements of the black middle class or about unusual persons, such as a 70-year-old black man who carves wooden armies and recreates Civil War battles with them. One of the aims of the newspaper study reported here was to ascertain whether the coverage of American blacks presented after the confrontations of the civil rights movement dwindled had begun to include this more varied and balanced kind of portrayal.[19]

NATURE OF STUDY

The most accurate method of determining how press coverage of black Americans has changed since the civil rights movement would be to conduct a detailed analysis of coverage by a large number of newspapers since 1960, but such a project was beyond the scope of this work. Instead, four major metropolitan newspapers located in different parts of the country were chosen for examination, and their coverage of black Americans was analyzed.

The findings concerning their reportage on black Americans cannot be claimed to be representative of that of the nation's news media in general. However, since keen competition among the various news media leads them to monitor each other's output closely and influences them to set similar agendas for news coverage, the performances of the four leading newspapers studied in this project may suggest coverage approaches to be found in other media as well. The papers studied were the *New York Times*, the *Chicago Tribune*, the *Atlanta Constitution*, and the *Boston Globe*.

A major concern of the study was to try to ascertain whether the newspapers' coverage of American blacks in the 1970s seemed to give evidence that the papers had begun to implement the suggestions for coverage improvement raised by the Kerner Commission and the journalists' own self-examination in the late 1960s. Thus, some primary questions to be answered by the research were: "What progress did the papers make in the 1970s in their coverage of blacks?" and "What coverage improvements remain to be made?"

The papers' racial coverage during the 1960s was also analyzed, for two reasons. One was to provide a basis for comparison of the coverage during the 1970s; another was to try to ascertain empirically whether the coverage criticisms made by journalists, the Kerner Commission, and others were valid. In addition, the four newspapers' coverage of American blacks during the early 1950s was sampled to gain some indication of the papers' treatment of news about blacks before the confrontations of the civil rights movement commanded media attention.

Besides the systematic analysis of samples of press coverage of black Americans in four leading newspapers between 1950 and 1980, this book also includes several other vital sources of information covering this topic. During the late 1960s, when the subject was extensively examined by journalists and others concerned, their conclusions were reported in assorted conference reports and articles in professional periodicals. Additional information on the topic was available in scattered studies made earlier by scholars and in the Kerner report's section on the media and race relations. In this work an attempt has been made to draw together the conclusions from these various sources, to extract the criticisms common to all of them, and to analyze why these coverage deficiencies occurred.

The discussions of minority coverage after the civil rights movement also were reported in scattered sources, and many of them have been assembled here, along with reports of the few scholarly studies of coverage of American blacks done since 1970. The results of the discussions and studies from that period are compared to the criticisms voiced in the previous decade to see which coverage problems remain, whether any new ones have appeared, and which suggested coverage improvements have been implemented. The study of coverage in the four leading papers provides empirical evidence of the earlier coverage criticisms, of the improvements made, and of those remaining to be made.

Also, the many ideas for improving coverage of American blacks and of race relations proposed during both decades have been consolidated here. These suggestions, particularly those made during the 1960s conferences, represent some of the most creative thinking done on this subject and offer some valuable ideas well worth retrieving and considering further.

In addition, a realistic appraisal of the media's role in relation to the American racial situation seems necessary. During the late 1960s the media were frequently castigated by observers and even by journalists themselves for the deficiencies of their coverage and for their failure to assume greater leadership in informing citizens of the problems facing American blacks. Great potential for effecting social change was ascribed to the media. Although to some extent these criticisms and claims were valid, it would be helpful to examine in greater detail some of the built-in limitations of the media's coverage of racial matters and to attempt to appraise realistically the media's power to make a difference in relations between the races.

Several factors suggest that further examination of techniques for reporting the situation of American blacks would be valuable. As the socioeconomic data mentioned earlier indicate, the nation's racial crisis is by no means resolved, even though dramatic conflicts have seldom occurred of late. Improved newspaper coverage that informs and educates white Americans about the lives and concerns of black citizens might serve to improve communications between the races and thereby reduce racial tensions. Ideally, it might also arouse citizens to press for reforms to alleviate injustices. Thus, a study that helps provide information about how the press has failed in its coverage of racial problems, and how it can perform better, can be useful.

Finally, the question of media coverage of minorities is one that perennially concerns communications scholars. This study, by helping to pinpoint coverage deficiencies and consolidate suggestions for improvements, may provide some guidelines on how the press could more adequately cover various racial and ethnic groups. Examples that spring to mind are Hispanics, Asian Americans, Native Americans, migrant workers, and the elderly. Persons representing each of these groups have complained that their lives, concerns, and culture are underrepresented in the media.

Despite the criticisms included in this book, it is not the author's aim to castigate the news media for either past or present inadequacies in their coverage of black Americans and race relations. Instead, the book's purpose is to point out coverage deficiencies, using both observers' comments and systematic analysis of the coverage, to discuss why the deficiencies occurred and to present suggestions for ways the coverage could be improved.

In fairness, it should be noted that despite inadequacies in their coverage, the media helped considerably to advance the civil rights movement of the 1960s, and in the ensuing decades they have made efforts to redress their past inattention toward blacks. During the 1960s the extensive and graphic portrayal of racial violence by whites in Birmingham and Selma and other southern communities provided by the media, especially television, shocked the nation into a realization of the oppression and hostility endured by blacks in the

South. Simultaneously, articles and editorials in hundreds of newspapers reminded readers of American society's ideals of equality and justice and pointed out the huge gap between these ideals and the reality of life for many black Americans.

After the ghetto uprisings forced the nation to realize that racial oppression and inequality were not confined to the South, many newspapers turned their attention to the ghettos of their own cities and began investigating and reporting on conditions there. Notable among the efforts of this period were the special sections produced by the *Los Angeles Times* and the *Detroit Free Press* and the November 20, 1967, special issue of *Newsweek* on "The Negro American— What Must Be Done."

Since that time many media have made a strong commitment to bring more minority reporters into journalism, have tried to improve their coverage of black concerns, and have made a conscious effort to become more sensitive and knowledgeable about racial issues. In the early 1980s, several perceptive in-depth studies of the state of black Americans were published by the Gannett News Service and the *Wall Street Journal*, among other newspapers.

It should be noted that the coverage inadequacies ascribed to the media in the following chapters are discussed as though they were committed by *all* media, although clearly many individual exceptions and differences exist. One cannot, with accuracy, attribute certain behavior to "the media" when there are so many variations among media. News is covered and presented by television in a very different manner than it is by newspapers, and practices among newspapers vary also from those in radio and news magazines. In addition, vast differences exist among representatives of each kind of media. For example, during the civil rights decade the assumptions underlying news treatment of race at the Jackson, Mississippi, *Clarion-Ledger*, were vastly different from those operating at the *New York Times*.

In addition, "the media" include many black-owned newspapers, magazines, and broadcasting stations across the country that cover the activities and problems of black Americans, explore contributions of blacks, and expose racial injustices. For over one hundred years the nation has had a small but vigorous black press that has been especially active in providing leadership in the struggle for black equality. But the overwhelming majority of the nation's mass communications media are owned and staffed by whites, and these media are the subject of this study. Because of the differences among media, the attitudes and deficiencies discussed in the following chapters are intended as descriptions of general situations. They do not apply to each individual medium, nor are they necessarily true for the whole thirty-year period under discussion. Instead, they describe prevalent general situations among white American news media.

Before the problems of press coverage of black Americans are discussed, it would be useful to analyze more carefully just what responsibility the press can realistically be expected to undertake in the reporting of the nation's racial situation and what kinds of coverage could be considered adequate. These matters are discussed in the next chapter.

NOTES

1. *Report of the National Advisory Commission on Civil Disorders* (New York: New York Times Co., 1968), pp. 363, 383.
2. Jack Lyle, "Introduction," in Lyle, ed., *The Black American and the Press* (Los Angeles: Ward Ritchie, 1968), p. xv.
3. Lawrence Schneider, *The Newsman and the Race Story* (Seattle: Univ. of Washington School of Communications, 1968), p. ii.
4. *National Advisory Commission*, p. 384.
5. Ben W. Gilbert, "An Extraordinary Indictment of the Press," *ASNE Bulletin*, April 1968, p. 14.
6. Woody Klein, "News Media and Race Relations: A Self-Portrait," *Columbia Journalism Review* 7, no. 3 (Fall 1968), 42.
7. Lyle, "Introduction," p. xii.
8. "One Nation, Divisible?," in Gannett News Service special report, *Equality: America's Unfinished Business* (Fort Myers, Fla.: News Press, 1981), p. 4.
9. Data is from Irving J. Sloan, ed., *The Blacks in America, 1492–1977: A Chronology and Fact Book*, 4th ed. (Dobbs Ferry, N.Y.: Oceana Publications, 1977), p. 141; Gannett News Service, p. 21.
10. Data is from Sloan, p. 144; Gannett News Service, p. 4.
11. Data is from *National Advisory Commission*, p. 255; Charles P. Alexander, "Bad Tidings for the Jobless," *Time*, 13 Dec. 1982, p. 54; Pamela Douglas, "The War on Black Children," *Black Enterprise*, May 1981, p. 25.
12. Data is from Sloan, p. 154; Gannett News Service, p. 4.
13. Gannett News Service, p. 20.

14. Data is from Sloan, p. 157; Douglas, p. 27.

15. Gannett News Service, p. 3.

16. Charles W. Stevens, "Integration Is Elusive Despite Recent Gains; Social Barriers Remain," *Wall Street Journal*, 29 Sept. 1980, p. 1, col. 1.

17. *National Advisory Commission*, p. 383.

18. Ibid.

19. The black struggle for equality was of course in progress well before the mid-1950s, and is still continuing, but for purposes of this study the civil rights movement is considered to be that period of the struggle which occurred in the late 1950s and all of the 1960s, and which was characterized by confrontational direct action and progress on the federal level toward securing civil rights.

CHAPTER 2

The Media's Role
in Race Relations

"It is the responsibility of the news media to tell the story of race relations in America," the Kerner Commission claimed, and the media executives responding to the survey mentioned earlier seemed to agree. But *do* the media have such a responsibility? Why? How can such a job be ascribed to "the news media," as though they comprised a single organization with one directing administration?

During the UCLA conference, one participant, discussing the Watts riot, said, "The news media have been remiss because they have not provided our society with any warning signals. They have not told white people what [ghetto] conditions were and are. This resulted in violence, and when the violence came it was not understood."[1]

Communications educator William Rivers expressed a similar idea during the late 1960s. Referring to the ghetto riots, he said, "We might not now be experiencing such a cataclysmic period, had the news media alerted us to the pitiful conditions of Negro life decades ago. At the very least, journalistic explorations of ghetto existence would have enabled us to understand the violence that accompanies the modern demand for civil rights."[2]

These comments carry a double message. Implicit in the remarks is the idea that if the media had done a better job of exposing the conditions of ghetto life, the riots might have been averted. But do the news media really have this kind of power? If they had portrayed more clearly to white audiences what the Kerner Commission described as the hopelessness and degradation of living in the ghetto, would their audiences have cared? Would anything have been done about ghetto living conditions?

The other message in the remarks just quoted is that more media attention to the conditions of ghetto life would at least have enabled white audiences to understand the violence that resulted from continued denial of equality to blacks. But is increased understanding enough? A careful examination of these questions and the issues surrounding them is a necessary prerequisite to a meaningful discussion of the problems and performance of the media in covering American blacks and race relations.

MEDIA RESPONSIBILITY

It is commonly accepted by both media representatives and observers that the media have some responsibilities to American society arising from the special protection they are given under the First Amendment to the Constitution, which states that Congress shall make no law abridging the freedom of the press. Newspapers, along with radio and television, are called the Fourth Estate, reflecting the belief that in a democratic form of government the news media constitute one of the bodies representing the people. In communications theory, their role is to serve as a watchdog on government and to provide citizens with the information they need to choose elected representatives and to make informed decisions on matters of public concern.[3]

In this century, still another idea has been added to the concept of the media's role in American society. As Harry Stein and John Harrison have pointed out, one of the responsibilities frequently ascribed to the twentieth-century American press, by both observers and journalists themselves, is the role of keeping a watch on the health of American society and informing the public about serious social ills.

This philosophy, which underlies the media criticisms mentioned earlier in this chapter, is based on a belief that a democratic society has a self-correcting capacity. It holds that if the public is fully informed about corruption, injustice, or oppression in America, citizens may become aroused and agitate for reforms.[4] The belief was most noticeably displayed by the muckrakers of the early twentieth century and, later, by the post-Watergate investigative reporters of the 1970s. Muckrakers of both periods, as well as those who carried on the tradition of investigative journalism in the intervening half-century, shared, according to Stein and Harrison, "a faith in the ultimate rationality of men and women to make changes once confronted with full documentation of human and institutional error and defect."[5]

Thus, the Kerner Commission's assignment of responsibility to the media to tell the story of race relations in the United States is not so unreasonable as it might at first seem, because American journalism has a long tradition of responsibility to society. It also, in this century at least, has been expected by both observers and journalists themselves to serve as a watchdog on society's health. This expectation is embodied in the social responsibility concept of the press, which holds that the press, because it enjoys certain freedoms under the American form of government, is obligated to be responsible to society by providing citizens with information and debate on public affairs and by enlightening the public by providing the information it needs to make it capable of self-government.[6]

This set of beliefs was developed among journalists themselves during the early part of this century but was first drawn together and formally stated by the Commission on Freedom of the Press after World War II. The commission, also known as the Hutchins Commission, presented a list of five responsibilities to society which it said a free press should undertake to fulfill.

These were: (1) providing a truthful, comprehensive, and intelligent account of the day's events in a context which gives them meaning; (2) providing a forum for the exchange of comment and criticism; (3) projecting a representative picture of the constituent groups in society; (4) presenting and clarifying the goals and values of the society; and (5) providing a full access to the day's intelligence.[7]

These precepts parallel many of the expectations of media coverage expressed by the Kerner Commission and journalists and suggest that the principles of the social responsibility concept of the press could be applied to coverage of blacks and of racial problems.

For example, the Hutchins Commission stated, in presenting its first requirement, that "it is no longer enough to report *the fact* truthfully. It is now necessary to report *the truth about the fact*."[8] This contention reflects the concern expressed by journalists and Kerner Commission members who said they believed the press had done a good job of covering the *events* of both the civil rights movement and the urban riots but had largely failed to discover and explain the causes underlying each.

In its second injunction, that the press should provide a forum for the exchange of comment, the Hutchins Commission said "all the important viewpoints and interests in a society should be represented in its agencies of mass communication." If this is not done, the commission said, "the unchallenged assumptions of each group will continue to harden into prejudice" and groups within society will remain insulated from each other.[9] An echoing note was struck by the Kerner Commission's statement that the absence of black concerns and black faces from newspapers contributed to the white lack of understanding of black Americans and helped widen the gap between the two races. The commission's claim that the media unconsciously reflected the biases and indifference of white society toward blacks also is pertinent here.[10]

In its third requirement, the Hutchins Commission called for projection of a representative picture of the groups within society. The commission noted that people often make decisions in terms of favorable or unfavorable images, and it said that when the images portrayed by the mass media fail to present the social group realistically, they tend to pervert judgment.[11] Very similar is the concern expressed by black citizens and journalists over a newspaper tendency to perpetuate stereotypes of black Americans, to run news of blacks "only when they get in trouble with the law, or the welfare department," and to fail to cover the black community.[12]

The Hutchins Commission members believed, they said, "that if people are exposed to the inner truth of the life of a particular group, they will gradually build up respect for and understanding of it."[13] A related point is made by Paula Johnson, David Sears, and John McConahay in their study of coverage of blacks in Los Angeles newspapers. They suggest that more, and more accurate, newspaper coverage of the lives and concerns of black citizens could help to reduce racial oppression. "Experimental studies have consistently shown that the tendency to harm, exploit or take advantage of others is reduced by greater information about them," the authors state.[14]

In its fourth requirement, the Hutchins Commission said that a free society requires of its press a clarification of the goals of the society, including "realistic reporting of the events and forces that militate against the attainment of social goals as well as of those which work for them."[15] Here again, newspaper coverage of American blacks and of race relations provides an example of the possible application of the social responsibility principles to a specific social problem.

Clearly, one of the stated goals of American society is equality of justice and opportunity for all citizens. If the press fails to report on the forces that prevent black Americans from experiencing these benefits, other members of society are unlikely to realize that problems exist. As Eric Blanchard wrote in reference to hunger in America, "Unless we can read in our national press about the violence to the poor that comes from starving for a full stomach, equal treatment, and a reasonably secure future, we will remain ignorant and will be frightened of their certain and predictable wrath."[16]

The final requirement stated by the Hutchins Commission was a full access to the day's intelligence. This requirement is based on the commission's belief that all citizens should be provided with current information and opinion, especially since leadership in American society is constantly changing and today's citizen could assume a leadership role tomorrow.[17] In the specific case of the problems of black Americans, especially those living in urban ghettos, citizens and potential citizen-leaders must be made aware that problems exist and that solutions are needed before reform is likely to occur.

PROBLEMS OF APPLICATION

Although application of the tenets of the social responsibility philosophy would seem an effective method of producing the kind of coverage of racial matters urged by the Kerner Commission, several serious obstacles to such a course of action exist. One of these is that while most journalists agree in theory with the standards of newspaper responsibility outlined by the Commission on Freedom of the Press, no acceptable procedure for implementing the standards has been found.

As John Merrill has pointed out, the social responsibility theory implies that some group, presumably one outside of journalism, is capable of defining what is socially responsible.[18] But journalists have long been hostile to any possibility of outside regulation. In fact, their extreme aversion to any threat to their autonomy—even by fellow journalists—is illustrated by the dearth of press councils around the nation and the demise of the National News Council. A *probs* few state and regional press councils exist, but they lack enforcement powers, as did the National News Council, which was formed in 1973 and disbanded in 1984 without ever having won wide acceptance among news organizations.

Although American newspaper personnel have successfully resisted all suggestions for outside regulation of the press, the situation among the broadcast media is somewhat different. The Federal Communications Commission (FCC), through its licensing authority over individual radio and television stations, has had the power to enforce adherence to FCC regulations that demand at least a minimum of responsibility to the public. But the impact of cable television on the broadcasting industry is influencing the FCC toward deregulation and a relaxing of FCC criteria for local stations' performance. Local broadcasters are now under even less pressure than they once were to demonstrate community responsibility and public service commitment.

Besides the autonomy of the American press, another factor militates against the implementation of the social responsibility philosophy of the press and of the Kerner Commission's charge. This is the multiplicity of media ownership in the United States and the lack of any central organization that serves all media and that could disseminate information about the tenets of the responsibility concepts and monitor media performance in these areas.

An example of this situation may be seen in the matter of hiring minority journalists. One of the strongest recommendations of the Kerner Commission, in its report on the mass media and race relations, was that the media seek out, hire, and promote black journalists to counteract the media's all-white perspective and to project the black community to white audiences.[19] This course of action was urged in every mass media/race relations conference held in the late 1960s, and many newspapers actively sought black reporters to cover ghetto uprisings and the developing race relations story.

Yet in 1972 the ASNE reported that members of minority groups still comprised less than 1 percent of the nation's news force.[20] The *stats* ASNE continued to monitor the situation and encourage the hiring of minority journalists. By 1982, although the situation had improved and minorities represented 5.5 percent of newsroom employees, only a handful of these held executive positions, 60 percent of the nation's newspaper staffs remained all white, and obstacles to minority hiring and promotion remained strong.[21]

It seems clear that even the efforts of one of journalism's most respected and influential professional organizations have not been sufficient to effect major change in the way American newspapers hire and—indirectly—cover minorities. And, of course, the ASNE's work does not even begin to affect television, where black reporters are more visible than they were in the 1960s but are almost completely excluded from positions of power.[22]

Although considerable consolidation has occurred in the communications industry with the growth of newspaper chains, and although three broadcasting networks are preeminent, the nation has thousands of individually owned daily and weekly newspapers and radio and television stations. Thus, it seems in a sense unrealistic to assign the task of presenting the story of the nation's racial situation to the news media, as though they comprised a monolithic group with a centralized authority that could enforce mediawide standards of coverage.

Another problem with implementing social responsibility concepts is that philosophical principles have a way of getting mislaid in the day-to-day operation of a newsroom. Probably many reporters and media executives who agree with the philosophy in principle do not often think about it as they make daily decisions concerning news coverage. In fact, some journalists may not even have heard of this philosophy, although they are aware, at least in a general way, that the media have a vital role in a democratic society to provide information needed by citizens. This is why reporters so often assert their right to gather news based on "the public's right to know."

Yet the journalist's responsibility to the public is not the primary factor determining how he or she does his or her job. Instead, he or she is most strongly influenced by the attitudes of superiors and colleagues and by the acceptance, status, and rewards he or she can acquire. As a factor shaping how and what a reporter writes, abstract considerations of social responsibility run a poor second to an editor's approval or displeasure, as any idealistic young reporter soon discovers.

Warren Breed, in a 1955 study based on interviews with numerous journalists, concluded that "the newsman's source of rewards is located not among the readers . . . but among his colleagues and superiors. Instead of adhering to societal and professional ideals, he re-defines his values to the more pragmatic level of the newsroom group," from whom he gets his rewards.[23]

In a 1960 study of how five California daily newspapers handled local civil rights and civil liberties stories, Walter Gieber pointed out the same situation. He suggested that journalists are not motivated by the social responsibility role so much as they are influenced by the pressures within their own newsrooms.

Gieber found that the factors affecting the reporters' handling of their stories were newspaper policy (both stated and unwritten), the bureaucratic structure and emotional climate of the newsroom, and the values held by the reporters' peers and superiors. Reporters are not oriented primarily toward their audience, Gieber wrote.[24] Therefore, even journalists who agree in principle that they have a responsibility to society, or a responsibility to inform the public about racial problems, may find little opportunity to carry out their intentions because of the demands of their job and pressures within the newsroom.

Another disadvantage of the Kerner Commission's charge is that it is, in a way, akin to setting the fox to guard the henhouse. The news media are largely owned and staffed by whites, all of whom have been tinged by racism to some extent because they live in a society in which color prejudice is deeply entrenched.

Paul Hartmann and Charles Husband, in their study of racism and the news media in Britain, point out that color prejudice is characterized by the belief that the white man is superior to the man of another color.[25] In America, this conviction has been advanced in varying forms to justify white Americans' theft of land from Native Americans, the treatment of blacks as objects rather than people during slavery and the subsequent oppression of blacks, and the exploitation of Chinese imported to work on the transcontinental railroads and of Mexican migrant workers. White Americans live in a society that from its inception has created an intricate system of rationalizations to justify inhuman treatment of people of another color for the white person's advantage. No white people, including journalists, can escape being affected by racism.

Hartmann and Husband observe that "prejudice resides in the culture." Although persons differ in the degree to which prejudiced assumptions color their outlook on the world and influence their actions, the authors say, it is "misleading to label people as prejudiced or unprejudiced as though prejudice were a purely personal characteristic" when they live in a society permeated by racist beliefs and imagery. The authors also note, in words that could apply to the United States as well as to Britain, that "racist ideas and the officially endorsed values of democracy coexist in British culture."[26]

Because color prejudice is endemic to American society, journalists are affected by it and frequently express in news coverage and editorials the racist assumptions that are accepted in the white society of which they are part. The degree of this expression varies greatly, depending upon social norms, from one time period to another and in different parts of the country.

In his study of the racial attitudes of gatekeepers, Gary Norman Van Tubergen suggested that as a reporter joins a newsroom group, his or her racial attitudes move toward what he or she perceives to be the group's norm. One danger in this situation, Van Tubergen noted, is that when certain values or attitudes are widely held within a group, members of the group tend to make the assumption that "the attitudes are normal and universal, and make up some nebulous set of 'facts.'"[27] Thus, a newspaper's journalists who share the same general racial attitudes can come to feel that their attitudes constitute factual knowledge, especially if their beliefs seem to be shared by a large segment of the society in which they live.

Van Tubergen used as an illustration editorial statements betraying blatant racial bias that were run in Los Angeles newspapers after the "zoot suit riots" of World War II. In June of 1943, hundreds of U.S. servicemen roamed through Los Angeles for several nights attacking every Mexican-American youth they could find in retaliation for the beating of a sailor by a Mexican-American youth several nights earlier. The editorials in several Los Angeles papers enthusiastically endorsed the servicemen's behavior, and one stated, "It is too bad the servicemen were called off before they were able to complete the job."[28]

It is not difficult to find other examples besides Van Tubergen's of what would today be condemned as racial bias but which were apparently editorial expressions of the sentiments prevailing in the society—and among journalists—at the time. For instance, in 1893, after U.S. soldiers massacred every Native American woman, child, and warrior at Wounded Knee, South Dakota, many western newspaper editorials celebrated the soldiers' action and expressed unabashed their conviction that "the only good Indian is a dead Indian."[29]

Editorial expression of racial bias is by no means limited to periods in the nation's distant and less enlightened past. (A more recent example is some southern newspapers' editorial response to the 1954 U.S. Supreme Court school desegregation decision.) Andrew Secrest, in a study of editorials in South Carolina newspapers during the decade after the decision, found that several of the newspapers' editorials approved the action of white mobs that had successfully prevented voluntary desegregation in West Virginia and Delaware. The editorials also suggested that such disruptions might well be used by other southern communities faced with pressure to integrate their schools.[30]

Florence Mars, in her book describing the reactions of the white community of Philadelphia, Mississippi, to the events surrounding the discovery of the bodies of three murdered civil rights workers there in 1964, presents another recent example of newspaper coverage and editorials that mirrored the racist assumptions of the society the newspaper served. (The editorials reflected the white community's unwillingness to see the oppression under which local black residents lived, its indignation at federally ordered desegregation, its conviction that civil rights workers were bent upon stirring up trouble, its lack of compassion for the murdered youths, and its unwillingness to accept any responsibility for the murders.)[31]

Even when societal—and journalists'—attitudes toward racial matters change, problems may arise in efforts to express the new attitudes in press coverage. Each newspaper has in its organizational structure many levels of gatekeepers who may represent various racial attitudes and different degrees of sense of responsibility toward society. (It would be possible for an editor or publisher and possibly even a majority of the reporting staff to have an enlightened attitude toward race relations but for their efforts to be undermined in subtle ways by the wording of headlines on the copy desk or the juxtaposition of certain stories by the makeup room staff.)

As the foregoing discussion has indicated, even though the historical role of the press in American society provides some justification for the Kerner Commission's assignment of responsibility to the media for telling the story of race relations in the United States, many difficulties hinder the performance of such a task. One of these is the absence of a method for implementing this kind of coverage, because of the autonomy of the American press and the fragmented nature of media ownership. Another is the difficulty of translating social responsibility principles into action amidst the daily pressures of news reporting. Still another is the fact that many media owners and reporters are themselves racist, some unashamedly, and some unconsciously.

LIMITATIONS AND POTENTIAL OF MEDIA CONTRIBUTIONS

If by some miracle the media were somehow to be owned and staffed entirely by enlightened persons imbued with the determination to present to readers an accurate picture of black Americans and their problems in U.S. society, would their coverage make any real difference, in practical terms, in altering racist attitudes?

Several considerations suggest that the media's potential for effecting change in this area is limited. One of these is the experience of racially moderate southern newspaper editors in the decade following the 1954 Supreme Court school desegregation decision. Many editors who opposed the rabidly pro-segregation sentiments of the communities they served were subjected to varying degrees of punishment. Some were simply ignored and lost their effectiveness—and their advertisers. Others were attacked physically and their businesses burned.

Hugh Davis Graham, in his book on press coverage of desegregation in Tennessee in the 1950s and 1960s, noted the persecution and ostracism of several moderate newspaper editors in Mississippi during this period. He suggested that such situations serve as a warning to persons "who might be tempted to endow the press excessively with singular powers of persuasion."[32] *Atlanta Constitution* editor Ralph McGill, also a moderate, was frequently harassed for his editorial stands during this time.

Calvin Hernton observed of the South in the mid-1960s that "the pressures on whites to conform to the practices of racism are often as severe as those placed upon the Negro." He added that any southern white who displayed any attitude toward blacks other than the prescribed one of extreme bigotry was immediately labeled "nigger lover') and subject to all types of reprisals, including bodily harm.[33] These observations seem to suggest that editors whose racial attitudes vary considerably from those of the community they serve risk the loss of their effectiveness—and much more—if they present their views too forcefully.

[In areas of the country and in periods when passions are less aroused, media attempting a more responsible coverage of race relations might find their contributions only partially successful for another reason.] This is the human tendency to assimilate only that information that conforms to our inner picture of the world.

Hartmann and Husband, in their study of how the media affected racial attitudes in Britain, found that their respondents noticed and recalled information in the media that confirmed their existing attitudes toward other races. [For instance, those respondents with a high hostility score toward colored immigrants tended to recall newspaper articles about people of other races involved in crime, riots, trouble, and illegal immigration]. Those with low hostility scores, however, remembered items about prejudice against people of other races and the disadvantages under which they lived. The authors noted that the information the respondents recalled thus was of a kind to confirm their existing racial attitudes.[34]

More thorough and representative coverage of race relations could prove ineffective for still another reason besides the hostility of prejudiced readers. [Such coverage might simply be ignored by a public that was indifferent to the problems described or uninterested in seeking action to alleviate them.]

An example of this situation was described by James Bassett of the *Los Angeles Times* at the University of Missouri conference. According to Bassett, in the early 1960s, the *Times* published numerous pages—including two major reports—of in-depth investigations of the mounting problems in the city's black ghettos and committed manpower and newspaper space to the situation even when it was not officially a "crisis." Yet in 1965, the Watts riot, one of the first and worst of the 1960s ghetto uprisings, erupted in south Los Angeles, claiming thirty-four lives and causing $44 million in damages.[35] [Clearly, alleviating social problems requires much more than portrayal of the ills by the media. Exposure of the maladies must be followed by action urged by concerned citizens and implemented by lawmakers and other leaders.]

Carey McWilliams, editor of the long-established investigative journal *The Nation*, has stated that the public's response to muckraking and other types of reform journalism varies widely during different time periods. At some times members of the public seem sensitive to the information provided by investigative journalists and react vigorously, he says, while at others they do not seem interested in the investigative journalists' revelations.[36]

Despite the difficulties of achieving better coverage of racial matters, and the forces that limit its effectiveness, such coverage remains an ideal worth striving toward. Hartmann and Husband, even when noting that their respondents tended to remember media items that confirmed their existing attitudes toward race, suggested that "the media provide people with a picture of the world which makes the development of one kind of attitude more likely than another."

They suggest that although media may not directly affect people's attitudes about race, media play a significant part in shaping public consciousness on matters of race. In their content analysis of the treatment of race in four British newspapers between 1963 and 1970, Hartmann and Husband found that the coverage "tended to emphasize those aspects of the situation in which coloured people appear essentially as a threat and a problem." This emphasis, the authors conclude, encourages the development of attitudes of hostility rather than acceptance among the white population.[37]

Johnson, Sears, and McConahay, in their study of coverage of blacks in Los Angeles newspapers from 1892 to 1968, expressed a similar idea. Their findings indicate that little press attention was given to blacks during most of the period studied, and the authors suggest that the increased coverage that was focused on black militancy and racial conflicts during the 1960s "bears with it the potential for badly frightening a white population that is quite naive and inexperienced about blacks." They also suggest that black invisibility in the white press may have facilitated white exploitation of blacks by contributing to white ignorance of blacks as people and of their problems.[38]

Thus it seems that the nature of media coverage of blacks is indeed related to the development of certain kinds of racial attitudes. Coverage that fails to present blacks as a normal part of society and ignores both their contributions and their difficulties can reinforce among whites the attitudes already fostered by the de facto segregation of American society—unfamiliarity with blacks as persons, ignorance of their concerns, and exploitation of blacks through indifference. In addition, coverage that emphasizes racial conflict can contribute to white fear and hostility toward blacks. Therefore, even if the media cannot change racial attitudes directly, they can promote the development of more enlightened attitudes by providing coverage that informs and educates and, as the Hutchins Commission suggested, interprets groups within society to each other.

Hugo Young, a leading British journalist, writes,

> It is clear to students of race relations that there is a strong correlation between race reporting and racial attitudes among the public; that the newspaper treatment of race relations has an important bearing on the quality of race relations . . . hence, that newspapers, when dealing with race have a particularly delicate responsibility. . . . Newspapers have unusual opportunities to do good or do harm in the situation which they are reporting. . . . They cannot escape a central role in race relations.[39]

Harold Evans, former editor of the *London Sunday Times*, agrees and cites several cases in which inaccurate reporting has considerably damaged race relations. He mentions the printing of a rumor that women were being molested, which touched off a riot in India, and states that publication of false statistics and unverified allegations has contributed to racial tension in Britain. He adds,

> There has been enough research to suggest that there is a connection between race reporting and racial attitudes and behaviour. In some instances a direct causal connection can be shown between racial information and racial violence. Less dramatic but more insidious is the way the stereotype of a whole ethnic group can be created and absorbed, reinforcing an existing attitude or stimulating a new one.

Evans adds that he believes newspapers have effects on race relations at two levels. "By the information they select and display and the opinions they present, they have effect . . . on the creation of stereotypes or the stimulation to behaviour. Because of the volatility of the subject, they also have swift effect at government level on the creation of policy."[40] This latter point is one that Hugo Young also makes, claiming that when the British government's racial policies are in flux, the government is strongly affected by public opinion on racial matters.[41]

In this country, Carl Stokes has commented on the same phenomenon. Stating that the press has a vital role to play in promoting understanding of civil rights issues, Stokes observed that "it is difficult to overestimate the political power of the media in shaping national policy on large and volatile issues."[42]

In a plea for continued media attention to black concerns, Johnson, Sears, and McConahay wrote in 1971:

Racial oppression now comes more often from the indifference and inattention of apparently polite and well-meaning whites than from naked bigotry. Blacks as persons, and their grievances, are too easily put out of mind. Preoccupied with their own interests, even the most liberal of whites have been easily distracted from the faint signals emanating from the isolated ghetto.[43]

These observations raise again the question of whether white readers would respond positively if the media transmitted a clearer picture of black grievances and the frustrations of black ghetto life. It is possible, of course, that white readers would react with indifference or even resentment. On the other hand, no movement for alleviating social injustice can begin without public knowledge that the injustice exists. Many factors are needed for an effective reform movement, but informing the public of the existence of the problem is one of the prerequisites for reform.

And who will provide that information, if the media do not? Because of the media's autonomy, the information presented by the media is less likely to be regarded as biased than that provided by other organizations, and certainly their coverage can reach more citizens than most individual organizations could contact.

As an activist quoted by Stein and Harrison has observed, the press's exposure of social ills provides the "last avenue of protest before more drastic action."[44] A participant in the University of Missouri conference made the same observation. Commending media that were seeking out the voiceless and powerless and presenting their grievances, he noted that the ghetto riots provided "sufficient evidence that if people are not given the opportunity to communicate their sorrow and their rage through normal channels, they will find their voice in Molotov cocktails and disorder."[45] Although the media cannot alleviate social problems, they can help provide a voice to those victimized by such conditions and, perhaps, help create a climate conducive to reform.

NOTES

1. Beverlee Bruce, "Comment by Beverlee Bruce," in Lyle, *The Black American and the Press*, p. 74.

2. Michelle Bender, "The Black Community—Whitewashed in the News? Can Coverage Be Improved?" *American Press*, May 1968, p. 31.

3. Julian Harriss, Kelly Leiter, and Stanley Johnson, *The Complete Reporter: Fundamentals of News Gathering, Writing, and Editing*, 3rd ed. (New York: Macmillan, 1977), pp. 8–9.

4. Harry H. Stein and John M. Harrison, "Muckraking Journalism in Twentieth Century America," in Harrison and Stein, eds., *Muckraking Past, Present and Future* (University Park: Pennsylvania State Univ. Press, 1973), pp. 14–18.

5. Ibid., p. 18.

6. Fred S. Siebert, Theodore Peterson, and Wilbur Schramm, *Four Theories of the Press: The Authoritarian, Libertarian, Social Responsibility and Soviet Communist Concepts of What the Press Should Be and Do* (Urbana: Univ. of Illinois Press, 1956), p. 74.

7. Robert D. Leigh, ed., Commission on Freedom of the Press, *A Free and Responsible Press, A General Report on Mass Communication: Newspapers, Radio, Motion Pictures, Magazines, and Books* (Chicago: Univ. of Chicago Press, 1947), pp. 20–21.

8. Ibid., p. 22; emphasis original.

9. Ibid., pp. 24–25.

10. *National Advisory Commission*, p. 366.

11. Leigh, p. 26.

12. Ben W. Gilbert, "Race Coverage," *ASNE Bulletin*, Jan. 1968, p. 2.

13. Leigh, p. 27.

14. Paula B. Johnson, David O. Sears, and John B. McConahay, "Black Invisibility, the Press and the Los Angeles Riot," *American Journal of Sociology* 76, no. 4 (Jan. 1971), 718.

15. Leigh, p. 27.

16. Eric D. Blanchard, "The Poor People and the 'White Press,'" *Columbia Journalism Review* 7, no. 3 (Fall 1968), 64.

17. Leigh, p. 28.

18. John Calhoun Merrill, *The Imperative of Freedom: A Philosophy of Journalistic Autonomy* (New York: Hastings House, 1974), p. 91.

19. *National Advisory Commission*, pp. 384–85.

20. ASNE Committee on Minority Employment, Committee on Education in Journalism, "ASNE on Minorities," *Columbia Journalism Review* 11, no. 1 (May/June 1972), 51.

21. Nick Kotz, "Keeping Score," *Columbia Journalism Review* 17, no. 6 (March/April 1979), 24; William H. Henry III, "Double Jeopardy in the Newsroom," *Time*, 29 Nov. 1982, p. 90.

22. Michael Massing, "Blackout in Television," *Columbia Journalism Review* 21, no. 4 (Nov./Dec. 1982), 38.

23. Warren Breed, "Social Control in the Newsroom: A Functional Analysis," *Social Forces* 33, no. 4 (May 1955), 335.

24. Walter Gieber, "Two Communicators of the News: A Study of the Role of Sources and Reporters," *Social Forces* 39, no. 1 (Oct. 1960), 80–83.

25. Paul Hartmann and Charles Husband, *Racism and the Mass Media: A Study of the Role of the Mass Media in the Formation of White Beliefs and Attitudes in Britain* (Totowa, N.J.: Rowman & Littlefield, 1974), pp. 36–37.

26. Ibid., p. 36.

27. Gary Norman Van Tubergen, "Racial Attitudes of Gatekeepers," Diss. Univ. of Iowa, 1968, pp. 10–11.

28. Ibid., pp. 1–5.

29. Randall Hines, "Selected Press Coverage of Wounded Knee," Diss. Kent State Univ., 1974, pp. 22, 30.

30. Andrew M. Secrest, "In Black and White: Press Opinion and Race Relations in South Carolina, 1954–1964," Diss. Duke Univ., 1972, pp. 102–3.

31. Florence Mars, *Witness in Philadelphia* (Baton Rouge: Louisiana State Univ. Press, 1977), pp. 80–81, 97, 266–67.

32. Hugh Davis Graham, *Crisis in Print: Desegregation and the Press in Tennessee* (Nashville: Vanderbilt Univ. Press, 1967), pp. 314–15.

33. Calvin C. Hernton, *Sex and Racism in America* (New York: Grove Press, 1966), p. 100.

34. Hartmann and Husband, p. 94.

35. James Bassett, "Watts and the Need for Press Involvement," in Fisher and Lowenstein, eds., *Race and the News Media* (New York: Praeger, 1967), pp. 37–40.

36. Carey McWilliams, "The Continuing Tradition of Reform Journalism," in Harrison and Stein, *Muckraking*, pp. 120–21.

37. Hartmann and Husband, pp. 95, 146.

38. Johnson, Sears, and McConahay, pp. 718–19.

39. Hugo Young, "The Treatment of Race in the British Press," in *Race and the Press* (London: Runnymede Trust, 1971), p. 29.

40. Harold Evans, "A Positive Policy," in *Race and the Press*, pp. 42, 44–45.

41. Young, pp. 29–30.

42. John DeMott, "White Racism in the Newspaper," *The Masthead* 33, no. 4 (Winter 1981), 10.

43. Johnson, Sears, and McConahay, p. 718.

44. Stein and Harrison, p. 12.

45. Samuel Dalsimer, "The Justice of Persuasion," in Fisher and Lowenstein, *Race and the News Media*, p. 115.

CHAPTER 3

Difficulties of Covering Racial News

When media coverage of American blacks was discussed by professional journalists during the 1960s, criticisms centered around two types of weaknesses. One was coverage flaws resulting from the media's failure to live up to their own acknowledged reporting goals, and these will be discussed in the next chapter. The other was misrepresentations that seemed to grow out of traditional news values and reporting practices and the media's position in American society.

Journalists and media critics who have considered media coverage of race relations have suggested that the way journalists perceive news—as discrete events, and as controversy—tends to produce a distorted picture of black Americans and race relations, as does the way news is gathered and written—with reliance upon official sources and emphasis on objectivity. These traditional news values and news-gathering practices, although they have served American journalists and their audiences well for many decades, often seem to produce a kind of coverage that is detrimental to relations between the races. In addition, the media's economic nature and place in society seem to further inhibit the media's ability to present an unbiased portrayal of black concerns and racial matters.

NEWS AS EVENTS

Covering the story of this country's racial situation adequately would seem to require portraying the position of the black American still trapped in the inner city—including his difficulties in obtaining economic opportunity, equality under the law, adequate housing, education, and medical care. The different problems of the black middle class also would need illumination. But an obvious difficulty with this requirement is that because of the very nature of news, the media are oriented toward reporting events, not long-term situations.

Reporting textbooks usually define news as a report of a current event, an intelligence of happenings or activities. One text states that "the newsworthy development is one that disrupts or alters—or shows promise of altering—the status quo."[1] Yet in the case of the black American, the status quo is precisely the area that needs to be illuminated, in order for white Americans to understand better the situation and frustrations of black citizens and perhaps to work toward change.

A good example was the long-standing denial of voting rights to many southern blacks and the news media's reponse to this situation. After the Reconstruction era, blacks were systematically disenfranchised in many parts of the South. In 1890, some 190,000 blacks were registered to vote in Mississippi, but that year the state constitution was rewritten to require that a prospective voter be able to read and interpret the state constitution; the stipulation was used to strike black voters from the voting rolls. Sixty years later, the state had only 22,000 black registered voters.

In 1954, voters in the state passed a measure requiring that voters be able to read and interpret the Constitution. The effect of this new voting requirement and intimidation by Citizens Councils reduced the number of black voters still further to 8,000 by 1958.[2] In 1964, only about 2 percent of the potential black voters in Mississippi were registered, and in eight counties no blacks at all were registered.[3] Blacks who tried to register were subject to economic reprisals, physical intimidation, and death. This situation was, of course, known to many members of the press both in and outside the South, and they largely ignored it.

Early in the summer of 1964 several civil rights organizations sent hundreds of college students, both white and black, into various Mississippi towns to work on voter registration projects. One of them, a white woman named Sally Belfrage, wrote that many students understood they were going to Mississippi as sacrificial victims; "they recognized that publicity and federal involvement could be achieved only if the victims were white—in a state where the beating and murder of Negroes was endemic and a matter of no national interest." And the protest marches and the beatings of that summer *were* covered by national news media, as was the discovery of the bodies of three murdered civil rights workers that August near Philadelphia, Mississippi. Belfrage noted that when she and her co-workers learned of the bodies' discovery they knew there would be a nationwide public reaction, because two of the victims were white.[4]

While Belfrage's views about the importance of the victims' race to the events' news value may well be justified, another vital point is that the protest marches and the murders were *events*, which were relatively easy for reporters to cover because they fit into the definition of news in a way that the long-standing disenfranchisement of black voters did not. Using the traditional questions of his profession, the five W's and the H, a reporter could cover the protests and the murders in terms of "What happened? To whom? When? Where? Why? How?" But attempting to describe the stages, methods, and results of seven decades of black disenfranchisement would require considerably more time and research. The story also would be more difficult to write because it did not fit easily into the newswriting formula and it would be less dramatic.

During the University of Missouri conference, Samuel Dalsimer observed that before the 1954 Supreme Court school desegregation decision "the plight of the American Negro was not considered 'hard' news. It was a plight, not a story."[5] To some extent this assessment remains true today, because American journalism remains focused on the coverage of discrete happenings, of events; it is not geared toward reporting on long-standing situations unless they flare into violence or controversy.

Reporter Caryl Rivers comments,

Problems that affect the lives of disenfranchised groups may be constant and unrelenting, but news about them is not. "We did our story on starvation a year ago," an editor will say. People may indeed be starving, but he is concerned with something else—OPEC has raised its prices; the primaries are coming up.

In a related observation, Rivers notes,

News is event-oriented, and outside the ordinary: dog bites man—no news; man bites dog—that's news. But much of the information that affects disenfranchised groups is negative in nature: people don't get jobs, health care isn't delivered, funds for a shelter for battered women don't materialize. If editors are not perceptive enough to see that it may be more important when things don't happen than when they do, such vital information . . . does not get reported.[6]

In the *Handbook of Reporting Methods*, Maxwell McCombs, Donald Lewis Shaw, and David Grey point out that "it is not in the press that one often enough learns of deeply embedded social problems . . . and proposed solutions to the problems of the day." Likening social conditions to icebergs, the authors add, "Public affairs reporting, with its emphasis on discrete news events, typically describes only the tips of our social icebergs, and usually only when they are close to being major disruptive forces in our communities."[7]

Jack Lyle, editor of the book on the UCLA symposium, suggested that "the American press [has] tended to operate by what has been called a 'crisis philosophy.' Literally swamped by the pressures of covering today's news explosions, the journalistic staffs have had too little time to adequately investigate and report developments which are as yet only potential explosions."[8]

At the University of Missouri conference, a frequently heard comment was that "the news media respond quickly and with keen interest to the conflicts and controversies of the racial story but for the most part disregard the problems that seethe beneath the surface until they erupt in the hot steam that is a 'live' news story."[9]

Hartmann and Husband, in a discussion of the American news media and race, note:

The news media are predisposed to handling discrete events—a court case, a riot, a speech—which can readily be fitted to the time schedules of their production processes. Realities which are not independent . . . occurrences, but which are evolving, interdependent conditions and processes—like ghetto existence, poor education, exploitation on racial grounds—are not so suited to the format imposed on realities by the news media's routinized process of news collection and treatment.

As the authors point out, it is relatively easy for television to cover a ghetto riot, a highly visual event; "it is much more difficult to televise the underlying causes of racial disturbances."[10]

It should be noted that although covering an ongoing situation may be less easy for reporters than covering an event, it is perfectly possible for the media to cover situations—they do it constantly, in feature articles, series stories, and television documentaries. For instance, during the late 1960s, newspapers in many cities across the country carried multi-installment, in-depth studies done by their own reporters on topics such as their city's black community, or black schools, or blacks and the criminal justice system.

Even today, in the burgeoning lifestyle sections of the nation's newspapers, readers find stories on where to find the best pizza in town, or how to care for wicker furniture, or how to interpret body language. Stories like these require research and have no news value or dramatic qualities. Yet they are run because editors think they will appeal to a portion of the newspaper's readers—just as editors thought during the late 1960s that readers would or should want to know more about the lives of their city's black residents. And this brings up the question of whether readers today would be similarly interested in stories on, say, living conditions in black neighborhoods in the inner city. This matter will be discussed later in this chapter.

NEWS AS CONTROVERSY

Another problem of covering the racial story adequately within the framework of traditional reporting techniques is that it is conflict, not harmony, that is newsworthy. Journalism students are taught, and professional reporters know, that news is reportage about the unusual, the dramatic—controversy, violence, death. The ordinary activities of the majority of the nation's law-abiding citizens, black as well as white, are not the stuff of which news is made.

One reporting text lists the commonly accepted news values as conflict, progress, disaster, effects upon the community, prominence of persons involved, novelty, and human interest—that is, arousing emotions or identification in readers.[11] It is logical for the news media to focus on events displaying these qualities, because reports of such happenings can alert the community to social problems or the imminence of social changes. The professional journalist does not consciously analyze these values in covering a story, but he or she is aware, when covering an event such as Patty Hearst's kidnapping, which included several of these elements, that he or she has a "terrific story."

Although the traditional conception of news values affects coverage of whites as well as blacks, in the latter case it has several negative results. First of all, when the media habitually deal with race in terms of conflict, as participants in the Columbia conference claimed they did, they present an inaccurate picture of minority groups. At this conference, "The media were accused of focusing on conflict and pathology . . . of treating the 97 per cent of Negroes who do not riot as virtually non-existent."[12] This emphasis on conflict conditions white readers to perceive blacks as a threat and a problem.

Eric Blanchard commented on this same phenomenon in his discussion of the newspaper coverage of the 1968 Poor People's Campaign demonstration at the Supreme Court. He said:

Almost unanimously newspapers chose to emphasize the disorder almost to the exclusion of background on the Indians' problems. . . . The net impact of newspaper treatment of the demonstration was almost totally negative (presumably reinforcing the attitudes of those who believe that the poor are criminals and eroding the positions of others who aren't sure yet).[13]

That same year, at the University of Chicago Center for Policy Study's conference, Lawrence Pinkham stated, "The Negro in America lives, quite literally, beyond the pale, and the media convey little about him that does not reinforce prejudice and stimulate fear."[14] In a largely segregated society such as ours, where 56 percent of the black population still lives in inner-city neighborhoods, many white citizens have little meaningful personal contact with black people and depend upon the media for their picture of black life and concerns. When the portrayal to which they are exposed is largely negative, they naturally form a distorted picture.

Another result of the media's conflict orientation also was mentioned at the Columbia conference. "Probably the most frequently voiced criticism [in a workshop on reporting the racial crisis] was that the media covered the ghetto only in terms of crime or racial crisis—a practice which, it was felt, made ghetto people think violence was the only way to get attention."[15] Other sources also have mentioned that the media's focus on violence leads disenfranchised groups to believe the only way they can attract public attention is through some sort of conflict. In addition, the journalistic focus on conflict favors the extremist of either race, who can capture media attention with verbal violence.

At the Columbia conference, "editors were charged with killing or not attempting positive human interest stories . . . that might correct the perspective of white readers who see race wholly in terms of conflict. The normal, day-to-day workings of the ghetto were thought to be inadequately reported. ('The general community doesn't know we get born, marry or die.') That . . . tended to make the Negro look like an abnormal character . . . with no existence outside riot or sports stories."[16]

In a similar vein, Martin Hayden observed at the University of Chicago conference that the media have not adequately told the story of ghetto problems.

Too many middle-class whites still assume that a great mass of Negroes enjoy a high, wide, and handsome life on public welfare. Too general is the presumption of whites . . . that Negro women willfully breed babies to get bigger checks. There is widespread failure to accept that the able-bodied Negro lounging on a street corner may well have job procurement problems other than simple shiftlessness.[17]

It is worth noting that although this observation was made in 1968, the stereotype to which it refers is still widely held by middle-class whites today. This is partly a result of the segregated nature of American society and partly an indication of the media's continued failure to explain adequately ghetto problems.

Again, it can be observed that the media, particularly newspapers, frequently run accounts of events and situations that are not negative. One of the traditional news values is progress, and while progress in race relations or civil rights is usually more long-term and less dramatic than man's first walk on the moon or a successful heart transplant, it is equally valid as a topic for coverage. However, because race relations seem often to be viewed by members of the press in terms of a problem, positive stories in this area seem to be uncommon.

At the Columbia conference, "much time was spent on the question of why good news about minority groups isn't news—for example, why the contribution of school integration to the education of all American children has not been properly spelled out in the mass media."[18] A similar situation was noted by Hartmann and Husband, who observed that race was covered in the British media with the same emphasis upon events and conflict that prevailed in the United States, and they stated that the media failed to point out to the public the advantages accruing from colored persons living in Britain.[19]

Related to this situation was Hartmann and Husband's observation of a tendency among both British and American journalists to perceive news about race within certain frameworks and to ignore events that do not fit into those frameworks. For example, their analysis of race-related material in four British newspapers between 1963 and 1970 revealed that the papers' coverage of race overseas centered on oppression, injustice, violence, and conflict between the races. Material about race in Britain also emphasized controversial themes; the authors believed that items that could be handled in these terms were more likely to be printed than those that could not.[20] The U.S. news media also may tend to cover race-related news that centers around certain dominant themes and to play down or ignore events that do not fall within this framework.

Georgia newspaper editor Sylvan Meyer noted this kind of framework when he discussed the way the press, in both North and South, covered the southern school desegregation crisis in the second half of the 1950s. The press consistently gave extensive coverage to any prominent Dixiecrat who damned the Supreme Court and urged "massive resistance" to federal encroachment on states' rights, Meyer wrote, although their speeches changed little between 1955 and 1959.

By emphasizing racist bombast and failing to explore possible approaches to school desegregation or to provide coverage of moderate sentiments, the press "let its preconceived notions strengthen myths that didn't exist and kill constructive reports before they could be aired simply because such statements didn't fit the pattern of the hour," Meyer stated.[21]

Other writers also have noted that the media's conditioned response to controversy allows extremists to capture headlines. During the 1960s, Whitney Young of the Urban League charged that the black protest movement was hampered by "the irresponsibility of the press and television." Young noted that many little-known black leaders were moved to make extreme statements in the knowledge that by this means they could attract media attention. "Yet at the same time," he said, "the carefully worked out programs for social change by the established organizations go unreported."[22]

Clearly, American journalism's emphasis on news as events, and as controversy, helps to produce a distorted picture of race relations and of American blacks. And this is the kind of news presented on the front pages of newspapers and on nightly television and radio newscasts.

But it should be noted that newspapers—and to a smaller extent TV and radio—offer their audiences much more than news. They also provide educational and human interest features, opinion, entertainment, and information about organizational and community activities. In these other kinds of material they have the opportunity to illuminate long-standing situations, explain causes of social problems, cover the activities of the black community, and delineate the enrichment of both races that is accomplished by successful instances of integration. Despite the pressure of the day's news events, media executives have the means at hand to present a more adequate picture of race relations that can be achieved by simply covering current race-related confrontations.

EMPHASIS ON OBJECTIVITY, RELIANCE UPON OFFICIAL SOURCES

Still another aspect of traditional journalistic values which helps distort reporting about race is, oddly enough, the American reporter's devotion to objectivity. Journalists are taught to take a neutral tone in their reporting, to keep their own opinions out of the story, to present both sides of an issue, and to limit their coverage to facts. But sometimes facts alone cannot present the whole truth of a situation, as the Hutchins Commission noted.

In the traditional view of journalism, the newspaper serves as a mirror for society; if the image presented in the mirror is ugly, that is because society is ugly, journalists say. The reporter's only obligation, the tradition holds, is to present the facts. But British editor Harold Evans states that this view is simplistic. "Facts may be sa-

cred," he says, "but which facts? The media are not a neutral look-
ing glass; we select what we mirror. We cannot help doing that. We
select what stories we will cover. We decide how much space or time
we will give and what display. . . . It is not enough to rely on the
accuracy of the facts assembled. We have to ask whether, as presented, they represent *truth*."[23]

This same point was remarked by *Chicago Daily News* executive
editor Lawrence S. Fanning at the University of Missouri conference, when he observed that "telling both sides of the story may
not always be telling the truth." He noted that when blacks in Selma
were quoted as saying that they were not permitted to vote and
newspapers simply printed the sheriff's denials of black disenfranchisement and then ended the story, the press had not advanced
readers' understanding. Some newspapers inserted a paragraph stating that almost no blacks were registered to vote in Selma, Fanning
noted, but he claimed that in such a situation it is vital for the press
to spell out that the public official is not telling the truth.

Touching upon a similar problem, Fanning noted that in the early
1960s blacks claimed that Negroes in Mississippi could not vote and
that most black children in northern cities went to all-black schools.
These were clearly demonstrable facts, Fanning noted, but some
newspapers reported them as though they were no more than un-
substantiated allegations, and such newspapers thus became agents
of those seeking to preserve the status quo. "When the media turn a
fact into an allegation," Fanning said, "they are not serving the truth
although, ironically, they may be serving the ethical traditions of
journalism."[24]

Hartmann and Husband note a report by Gaye Tuchman in
which she observes that in their efforts to achieve objectivity journalists use quotations from various sources as a means of removing
themselves from the story and providing "facts" to substantiate the
story. She notes that the quotations "relieved the reporter of responsibility for the views expressed even though he may have chosen the
quotation because it is what he would have liked to have said."[25]

Tuchman's comments illustrate one of the drawbacks in American
journalism's devotion to objectivity—namely, that this objectivity
involves numerous subjective decisions. The reporter must decide
which facts and quotations to use in his story and which to omit,
which to place high in the story and which to subordinate, which to

emphasize in the story's first paragraph. On a more general level, media executives make decisions about which stores are to be covered and which ignored, which are to be featured as the day's leading stories, and which of the major stories will receive top priority.

Reporters' devotion to objectivity was strongly attacked at the University of Washington seminar, where Lawrence Schneider said that "the time for hiding under the cover of objective reporting is over" because the problems of the day were too complex to be reported in this fashion. He said members of the press should recognize that objective reporting is based on a subjective notion that by quoting what various people said and "counting the number of marchers" a journalist is reporting adequately. "That is not so," Schneider said, "for beyond the simplest of stories, the reporter must offer insights into the causes of events if he is to communicate successfully regarding the event."[26]

Journalists are aware that their efforts to achieve objectivity involve much subjective decision making but have found no other method by which to strive toward the time-honored American journalistic tradition of objectivity and neutrality in reporting. Yet the system allows a lazy or uninformed reporter to produce a story that is factually accurate, and sounds objective, yet which is incomplete and gives the reader an entirely erroneous impression. More truly objective coverage is possible, of course, but requires a definite effort by the reporter to seek out the facts and the sources that will give the reader a more accurate picture of the situation.

In the matter of reporting about race perhaps a still more serious problem is the journalist's reliance upon official sources for facts and quotations. Members of the press develop routine contacts for news gathering, seeking information from official sources and recognized experts, and as a result the views of groups of persons with no formal organization or established leader frequently do not get reported. As participants in the Columbia University conference observed, the media tended to listen only to the establishment. Thus, the participants said, the media "would cover a routine mayoral proposal, but not the Freedom Budget."[27]

This overreliance upon official sources also was mentioned by the Kerner Commission, which reported that some editors and reporters acknowledged that during racial disturbances police and city officials were their main—and sometimes their only—sources of information.[28] At the University of Chicago conference, Edwin Diamond observed that "about the only time the white press reporters go into New York's Harlem or Detroit's Twelfth Street . . . is behind a police car when there is trouble."[29]

In such a situation, it is no wonder that the ghetto residents' lives, problems, and viewpoints were so little reported, as was charged by participants at all five conferences on the racial crisis and the media. Members of the Kerner Commission and participants at each of the conferences mentioned the need for reporters to develop more contacts within the black community, to learn the dynamics of the ghetto, and to cover routinely the activities of black organizations.

One of the strongest statements for the necessity of the media's moving beyond a narrow concern with facts and official sources to a presentation of the truth was made by journalist Jack Newfield, who wrote:

Objectivity can be defined as the way the mass media reported the history of the Vietnam War before the Pentagon Papers; the way the racism in the North was covered before Watts; the way auto safety was reported before Ralph Nader. . . . The goal for all journalists should be to come as close to the truth as possible. But the truth does not always reside exactly in the middle. Truth is not the square root of two balanced quotes.[30]

MEDIA ECONOMIC NATURE

A comment voiced by many participants in the Columbia conference was that the media catered too much to affluent white suburbanites.[31] But given the composition of the media's audience, and the nature of American media as business enterprises, this is not surprising. The media are, after all, funded largely by the advertising they carry, and advertisers are interested in reaching certain target audiences with the purchasing power to buy the advertisers' products.

As reporter Caryl Rivers has pointed out, media executives realize that in order to survive economically, they have to reach the affluent middle and upper classes, who are the major purchasers of information and the people the big advertisers want to reach. Thus, stories about the powerless and the disenfranchised tend not to be assigned, she says, because they are thought to have little appeal to such an audience.[32] As an executive of a large California daily said, "Look, we want to reach people who spend their weekends skiing, the couple that flies to London for a vacation. Our advertisers expect that kind of reader. They're not paying to reach poor people."[33]

While this may sound like a logical (if shortsighted) argument for not covering the poor, it is not, however, a good reason for not covering American blacks. In 1981, the purchasing power of the black middle class was $140 billion, making this group the ninth largest market in the world, and the figure is expected to increase by $7 billion a year.[34] Surely this is a group any advertiser would want to reach. If editorial content is indeed as influenced by advertisers' wishes as the previous argument would indicate, one would expect daily papers to be generously studded with articles about, or of interest to, the black middle class.

The argument has several other fallacies, also. Because of "white flight" to the suburbs over the past several decades, many urban newspapers are now in the position of having to reach out over the urban ethnic poor whom they are ignoring to reach the affluent suburbs where their target audiences live. And as the middle class moves farther away, the newspaper has to reach out further and further, meanwhile turning a blind eye to the concerns of citizens living just a few blocks from the newspaper office.

Although the urban poor generally do not read mass circulation daily newspapers, some real evidence by the newspaper of concern about their activities and problems might convert them into readers—a situation which could only be helpful to many financially beleaguered big-city dailies. In addition, suburban white—and black—readers need information about the frustrations and living conditions of residents of the ghetto, if they are to have a realistic picture of the society in which they live.

MEDIA POSITION IN SOCIETY

Another obstacle to accurate and adequate media coverage of black Americans, particularly those living in ghettos, is that the media are staffed largely by whites who are prevented by both race and class from understanding the tensions and oppression experienced by many blacks and from comprehending the nature of daily existence in the ghetto.

During the University of Chicago conference, Lerone Bennett, Jr., of *Ebony* said,

> White-oriented media cannot solve the race problem in America because white-oriented media are part of the race problem. They reflect the interests, values, and aspirations of white people. . . . So-called general media are white and are servants of white reality. They stand in an adversary relationship with the black community. They find themselves in the difficult position of reporting a court case to which they are parties.[35]

It should be noted that media bias is a class as well as a racial one. Reporters for American newspapers and broadcasting stations tend to be college-educated, to live in suburbs, and to make more money than many residents of the city their medium serves, while the owners of their newspaper or station usually enjoy a still higher status, moving in the same social and economic circles as the community's most influential leaders. And the larger and more prestigious the medium, the more exalted the position of its reporters and executives.

As Michael Novak has pointed out, "only a few Americans—national journalists among them—fly on airplanes, have expense accounts, are photographed with the glamorous and the powerful." It is these people, who constitute a subculture relatively unconnected with the average American, he says, who "guard the gates of the national media [and] determine what will be perceived by millions, from what angle, for how long. . . . What does not get 'out' in the national media might just as well—it sometimes seems—not exist."[36]

On a local level, white media owners and staffs have a similar monopoly on their audiences' perception of local affairs. It is perhaps not surprising when the picture they present is heavily influenced by their own interests and values and that minority groups become frustrated and angry at the paper's failure to cover their concerns or present their view of reality.

A related problem is the media's position as part of the white power structure of the nation. The Kerner Commission reported, after interviewing ghetto residents and middle-class blacks, that most persons they interviewed believed that the media are instruments of the white power structure and are guided by the interests of the white community.[37]

During the Columbia conference, a spokesman for a black power–oriented group claimed that the media "were not reporting his movement adequately because of the white power structure's fear of black power and its economic demands. A newsman agreed that advertisers do not like stories about black power leaders (or about the white poor)—with the result that editors often tone down such matter." Another participant said this situation was almost inevitable as long as the media were in the hands of wealthy corporations. Many participants also noted that news organizations, especially the smaller ones, "were loath to criticize business, government or the police because of their dependence on these news sources."[38]

In addition, because the media depend upon business interests for advertising, and upon local government and other power sources in the community for news, they are vulnerable to pressure from these groups. Often a local publisher or broadcasting station owner is a member of the same civic and social organizations as the community's most powerful citizens, so he can be subject to personal as well as monetary difficulties if he persists in running stories that these leaders feel are a threat to their interests.

A particular version of this problem was reported by Ted Poston at the University of Missouri conference. Describing the way a racially moderate Alabama newspaper editor had allowed his paper to become a publicity sheet for segregationists, Poston said the editor asked what else he could have done "in a small community like this when most of the important people in town had joined the White Citizens Council and when it had mustered a fifteen-thousand membership?"[39]

Hartmann and Husband state that color prejudice in British society serves the economic interests of the white power elite—the owners of capital—by maintaining a pool of cheap labor for menial work and also encouraging the economically exploited white to express anger in a manner harmless to the social system's beneficiaries by scapegoating colored immigrants, who are portrayed as a problem and a threat.[40] Although the authors' claims apply to Britain, certain parallels to American situations are obvious; racism may well serve similar functions in this society. American news media owners who are part of the nation's white power structure may have, however unconsciously, an economic interest in the maintenance of the racial status quo in the United States.

Besides reflecting a white outlook and values, white jo may also, as some researchers have claimed, tend to act as p of the status quo. Ways in which coverage can be slanted to present the least possible discomfort to the majority class were detailed by David Paletz and Robert Dunn in their study of local press coverage of a 1967 riot in Winston-Salem. The authors observed that the coverage concentrated heavily on measures to suppress the riot, displayed no understanding or sympathy with the rioters, and made little or no attempt to cover the story from the perspective of those engaged in the violence.

Thus, the coverage served to maintain sociocultural consensus, the authors said, by focusing on legitimate authority and its attempts to suppress lawlessness and by presenting those engaged in the disorders as atypical of local blacks. In the process, however, the coverage failed to explain to white readers the real concerns of the black community. The result of such coverage, the authors say, "is to protect power and class in the social structure. When riots occur, they are viewed as disruptions of consensus and threats to the community."[41]

Related to this situation is the fact that, because the media serve a largely white audience, their definition of what is newsworthy is tailored to the concerns of that audience. Hartmann and Husband state, "The day-to-day tensions of ghetto existence, and exploitation which is a crucial concern of the coloured population, are not a primary concern of the white public." Only when the symptoms of these conditions are expressed in events like picketing, demonstrations, and racial violence that impinge upon white consciousness, the authors say, do these events become newsworthy in a white press.

"One of the reasons for the inadequate coverage of the underlying causes of racial strain in the United States," write Hartmann and Husband, "is that the condition of the Negro is not in itself a matter of high interest to the white majority. Their interest in the black American is focused upon the situation in which he becomes a threat, or a problem."[42] Many other observers have commented upon this same phenomenon—the white media ignoring the most crucial concerns of the black man until he reacts to his situation in a way that threatens the interests or safety of whites.

Caryl Rivers points out still another problem involved in covering the disenfranchised. She says, "The nature of the career ladder inside media organizations is such that it steers talented people away from focusing on news of such groups." She adds that the most prestigious beats in the newspaper business are the political ones, and she says these are the jobs that lead to executive positions.

"If you are an ambitious young journalist," she writes, "you are well aware of the fact that you are not going to climb up the ladder of success by writing about kids who get bitten by rats, or neighborhoods flattened by expressways." Journalists like to be around people with power, she observes, and they know stories on such people can lead to prestige and promotion. "It's not exactly astonishing that reporters are not battling each other for the right to cover poor folks," she notes.[43]

The Kerner Commission, when it charged the media with viewing the world from a white man's perspective and failing to include blacks in its vision of America, highlighted the media's reluctance to accept the reality that ours is a multiracial nation.[44] At present, one American in five is a member of a minority race, and this percentage is steadily rising because of the great influx of Asian and Latin American immigrants to the United States in the early 1980s.

Yet the very complex ethnic mixture of American society has long been a reason for pride in this nation and has been considered a source of strength. Surely there is reason to expect that the nation's mass communications media would reflect our society's racial as well as ethnic diversity accurately in the picture they present of reality and would provide some perspectives different from those of the white majority.

Perhaps readers truly do not want to read stories about the poor and about social problems, as many advertisers and newspaper publishers claim. Yet it seems obvious that the press has at least a minimum responsibility to present readers with an accurate picture of the society in which they live. Surely a press that enjoys the power and constitutionally protected freedom that the American press does has some responsibility to society as well as to profits. Surely it is performing an actual disservice to comfortable middle-class white readers when it allows them to ignore the seething frustrations of inner-city residents, fails to present black perspectives of American society, and allows institutionalized injustices to flourish unreported.

A black participant at the University of Washington seminar said that "news is aimed at white middle-class America, which is the most isolated and least progressive class in the world. If they only get to read and see what they want to read and see, they are going to become even more isolated and egocentric, since the vast majority of the world is non-White and poor."[45]

It seems clear from the discussions quoted in this chapter that traditional news values and news-gathering practices, plus the media's economic nature and position in society, play a large part in producing inadequate and even harmful coverage of black Americans. It is obvious why Lerone Bennett said the white media are part of the race problem in the United States.

But it should be noted that these factors produce distorted coverage of other subjects and struggles besides those concerning American blacks. A George Washington University study of how ten leading American newspapers covered issues important to women between 1977 and 1982 traced deficiencies in the coverage to these same roots. The papers' conception of news as events led them to ignore situations affecting the lives of many women, the report said, while their focus on controversy produced misleading reportage and a neglect of important events where no conflict occurred. Because of their emphasis on confrontation and breaking hard news stories, "newspapers are missing some of the big, far-reaching stories of our times," the report stated.[46]

American diplomats and television journalists covering Central America in the early 1980s observed the same problems. The nightly news stories, they said, showed a jumbled montage of Central American scenes instead of a clear picture of the situation there, presented isolated events without any context to aid the viewers' understanding, and ignored vitally important stories for which no visuals were available.[47] In 1985, Hodding Carter III said traditional reporting practices hinder rather than help the public's understanding of foreign affairs and supply citizens with inadequate information on which to base informed decisions. He disagreed with newspaper surveys that show readers do not care about foreign affairs, saying that readers are turned away by the media's practice of bombarding them with "snippets" of news lacking context and background.[48]

The built-in problems described here are not unsolvable. A great deal could be achieved if media executives and journalists became more aware of—and began to guard against—the ways these factors can produce reporting that has a negative impact on race relations and that fails to provide citizens with adequate information to understand other important stories as well.

NOTES

1. Harriss, Leiter, and Johnson, pp. 22–24.

2. Mars, pp. 58–59.

3. Sally Belfrage, *Freedom Summer* (New York: Viking Press, 1965), p. 85.

4. Ibid., pp. 8, 180.

5. Dalsimer, p. 114.

6. Caryl Rivers, "Covering the Disenfranchised: A Working Reporter's Notes," in Rubin, ed., *Small Voices and Great Trumpets: Minorities and the Media* (New York: Praeger, 1980), pp. 55–56.

7. Maxwell McCombs, Donald Lewis Shaw, and David Grey, *Handbook of Reporting Methods* (Boston: Houghton Mifflin, 1976), pp. 5–6.

8. Lyle, "Introduction," p. ix.

9. Paul L. Fisher and Ralph L. Lowenstein, "Introduction and Guidelines," in Fisher and Lowenstein, *Race and the News Media*, p. 5.

10. Hartmann and Husband, pp. 157–58.

11. Harriss, Leiter, and Johnson, p. 29.

12. *Conference on Mass Media and Race Relations* (New York: American Jewish Committee, 1968), p. 9.

13. Blanchard, p. 62.

14. Lawrence Pinkham, "The Role of Public Television," in Daly, ed., *The Media and the Cities* (Chicago: Univ. of Chicago Center for Policy Study, 1968), p. 79.

15. *Conference on Mass Media and Race Relations*, p. 1.

16. Ibid., p. 9.

17. Martin S. Hayden, "A View from Detroit," in Daly, *The Media and the Cities*, p. 62.

18. *Conference on Mass Media and Race Relations*, pp. 8–9.

19. Hartmann and Husband, pp. 116–17.

20. Ibid., p. 144.

21. Sylvan Meyer, "The Press and the Schools," in Spearman and Meyer, *Racial Crisis and the Press* (Atlanta: Southern Regional Council, 1960), pp. 38, 43–44.

22. Anthony Lewis and the New York Times, *Portrait of a Decade: The Second American Revolution* (New York: Random House, 1964), p. 269.

23. Evans, pp. 42–43; emphasis original.

24. Lawrence S. Fanning, "The Media: Observer or Participant?" in Fisher and Lowenstein, *Race and the News Media*, pp. 111–12.

25. Hartmann and Husband, p. 158.

26. Schneider, *The Newsman and the Race Story*, pp. 4–5.

27. *Conference on Mass Media and Race Relations*, p. 2.

28. *National Advisory Commission*, p. 375.

29. Edwin Diamond, "Covering the Revolution," in Daly, *The Media and the Cities*, p. 26.

30. Jack Newfield, "Is There a 'New Journalism'?" in Weber, ed., *The Reporter as Artist: A Look at the New Journalism Controversy* (New York: Hastings House, 1974), p. 304.

31. *Conference on Mass Media and Race Relations*, p. 2.

32. Rivers, pp. 57–58.

33. Mel Mencher, "Journalism as Seen by Black Reporters and Students," *Journalism Quarterly* 46, no. 3 (Autumn 1969), 504.

34. Data is from Pamela Moreland, "Minorities—I: You Editors Make Me Angry," *ASNE Bulletin*, May/June 1982, p. 7; speech on "Blacks in the Media," by Greg Andrews, community affairs director of WYTV, at Black History Month program, Youngstown State University, Youngstown, Ohio, 21 Feb. 1983.

35. Lerone Bennett, Jr., "The White Media," in Daly, *The Media and the Cities*, pp. 7–8.

36. Michael Novak, "Why the Working Man Hates the Media," in Merrill and Barney, eds., *Ethics and the Press: Readings in Mass Media Morality* (New York: Hastings House, 1978), pp. 108–109.

37. *National Advisory Commission*, pp. 374–75.

38. *Conference on Mass Media and Race Relations*, p. 2.

39. Ted Poston, "The American Negro and Newspaper Myths," in Fisher and Lowenstein, *Race and the News Media*, p. 66.

40. Hartmann and Husband, pp. 206–7.

41. David L. Paletz and Robert Dunn, "Press Coverage of Civil Disorders: A Case Study of Winston-Salem, 1967," *Public Opinion Quarterly* 33, no. 3 (Fall 1969), 339–40, 345.

42. Hartmann and Husband, pp. 153–54.

43. Rivers, pp. 56–57.

44. *National Advisory Commission*, p. 383.

45. Schneider, *The Newsman and the Race Story*, p. 41.

46. Women Studies Program and Policy Center, George Washington

University, *A Newspaper Study: New Directions for News* (Washington, D.C.: George Washington Univ., 1983), pp. 2, 6, 11, 14.

47. John Weisman, "Why TV Is Missing the Picture in Central America," *TV Guide*, 15 Sept. 1984, pp. 4, 6, 8, 12.

48. Thomas Ott, "Hodding Carter Raps Foreign-News Coverage," *Youngstown Vindicator* (Ohio), 18 May 1985, p. 19.

CHAPTER 4

Past Deficiencies
of Coverage

As the previous chapter indicated, some of the deficiencies of media coverage of American blacks flow from traditional concepts of news and the way it is gathered and written, while other weaknesses arise from the nature of the media. But another group of coverage inadequacies can be traced to journalists' failure to live up to their own standards of good reporting, of neutrality, and of "holding a mirror up to society."

These deficiencies, discussed by journalists and the Kerner Commission during the second half of the 1960s, centered around several common themes. These were that the media had (1) failed to cover blacks as a normal part of American society and had instead presented the kinds of coverage that tended to promote stereotypes and reinforce prejudice; (2) failed to portray to their audiences the severe problems facing American blacks, especially ghetto residents; (3) failed to explain the causes and underlying conditions of black protest and instead focused on the conflict aspects of the civil rights movement; (4) tended to ignore local racial problems while emphasizing racial unrest in other locations; and (5) reflected in their coverage indifference and antipathy toward American blacks. Each of these coverage deficiencies has serious implications for race relations.

LACK OF EVERYDAY-LIFE COVERAGE

A complaint frequently voiced at the media/race relations conferences was that the news media consistently failed to present blacks as a normal, everyday part of American society. News about black organizations, achievements of individual blacks, even ordinary birth, marriage, and death news about blacks was generally ignored by newspapers, participants said, although the same kinds of news about white organizations and individuals was run.

At the Chicago conference, Ben Bagdikian commented that until the recent past, as far as the average white person knew, "Negroes did not go to school, earn scholarships, win election to the hierarchy of the Masons, attend PTA meetings, or die peaceful deaths after laudable or even uneventful lives." He wondered what effects this invisibility in the media had had on whites' perception of blacks and on the black man's perception of himself.[1]

In addition, news media were charged with acting as though the ghetto itself did not exist. Lacking sources in inner-city black neighborhoods and understanding of the dynamics operating there, journalists failed to cover not only the areas' problems but also their cultural, social, and sports events, said participants in the Columbia conference. The media were criticized for "picturing the ghetto as an area of idleness, ignorance, violence and lack of self-help. . . . The normal, day-to-day workings of the ghetto were thought to be inadequately reported."[2]

Early in 1968, *Washington Post* deputy managing editor Ben Gilbert noted that in the previous three months he had attended three meetings on press coverage of blacks. A recurring complaint voiced at the meetings, he said, was that few newspapers printed any news of the black community and organizations until problems developed. "Is it really true," he asked, "that we [the press] *are* just a branch of the power structure—the white one—and that we carry news about Negroes only when they get in trouble with the law, or the welfare department?"[3]

The press's ignoring of blacks also was stressed by the Kerner Commission. The world that newspapers and television portray is almost totally white, in both appearance and attitude, the commission stated. "Far too often," the commission claimed, "the press acts and talks about Negroes as if Negroes do not read the newspapers or watch television, give birth, marry, die, and go to PTA meetings."[4] The commission offered no supporting data, but earlier empirical studies made by scholars, to be reported later in this chapter, offer considerable support for the commission's contention.

The absence of black faces and activities from newspapers and television affects both blacks and whites, the commission claimed. It intensifies blacks' feelings of alienation and conditions whites to believe that blacks are not a normal, ordinary part of society, thus contributing to white lack of understanding and acceptance of black Americans. "By failing to portray the Negro as a matter of routine and in the context of the total society, the news media have, we believe, contributed to the black-white schism in this country," the commission said.[5]

Lawrence Schneider, in his report on the University of Washington seminar, observed that the civil rights movement and the riots forced white Americans to realize that they knew "virtually nothing" about black America. "They did not know Blacks as individuals, nor as a people with a special history, a special set of heroes, a special set of problems and a special life engendered by these problems."[6]

What was the reason for this inattention to black life and concerns on the part of the media? Some of it was probably an unconscious racism—a belief that blacks' activities and problems were not to be taken seriously—compounded by ignorance and indifference. In other cases it grew from a deliberate deference to racism in the society.

Pulitzer Prize–winner Ira Harkey said that until the early 1950s, the *New Orleans Times-Picayune* had a firm rule that blacks were not to appear in photographs it published, not even as part of a background. "Photos of street scenes were scrupulously scanned by picture editors and every perceivably black face was either excised by scissors or erased by air brush," Harkey notes.[7]

Clearly this is not the behavior of a newspaper concerned with accurately reflecting society. Instead, this kind of action bespeaks a willingness to distort reality in order to cater to its readers' sensibilities. A similar reluctance to accept reality may account for the treatment of colored immigrants in the British press. Hartmann and Husband say that "the essential feature of the press treatment of race [is that] coloured people have not on the whole been portrayed as an integral part of British society. Instead the press has continued to project an image of Britain as a *white* society in which the colored population is seen as some kind of aberration, a problem, or just an oddity, rather than as 'belonging' to the society."[8]

In this country, the media's ignoring of black Americans exposes

flimsiness of the argument of journalists who claim the
o responsibility in race relations except to "report the
..... hold a mirror up to society." In the past, the media have
been selective about which facts about blacks they reported and have
presented a distorted reflection of society—sometimes going to considerable lengths to do so.

STEREOTYPICAL COVERAGE

One of the chronic complaints at the 1960s conferences was that
what little attention the media did pay to blacks was negative and
was of the type to reinforce stereotypes. Blacks were consistently
portrayed as criminals, and news about crimes committed by blacks
often was given more play than similar crimes committed by whites,
the participants said.

Noting this fact, Bagdikian stated in 1968 that blacks of low status
and income were, like most low-status groups, often involved with
the law. "But this news treatment of blacks [as criminals] was more
persistent and more pernicious than that of any other low-status
group. And it was so in both the North and the South." He added
that among southern newspapers it had long been standard practice
to run all accusations of sex crimes against blacks on page one, even
if the paper had to reach thousands of miles to find a story. "To this
day," Bagdikian said, "it is possible to see played up on the front
page of the daily paper in Jackson, Mississippi, news of an obscure
Negro crime in Portland, Oregon."[9]

Another tendency in media treatment of blacks noted by conference participants was portrayal of blacks as shiftless and unreliable. Instances of welfare cheating by blacks were featured much
more than corresponding frauds by white welfare clients, the participants charged. In addition, they said, the proportion of blacks on
the welfare rolls was frequently emphasized in the media, even
though whites also get welfare and despite the fact that blacks' position at the bottom of the nation's socioeconomic ladder made it
inevitable that blacks would make up a large percentage of welfare
clients.

In addition, conference participants stated that the media's tendency to emphasize conflict had helped produce a picture of blacks

as dangerous. At the Columbia conference, participants criticized the media's sensationalism and asked why race was "habitually dealt with in terms of conflict." They added that the media too often consider only the negative to be newsworthy and consistently focus their leads on the most destructive aspect of a story. For instance, they said, the media always emphasized the most inflammatory remarks of black militants, ignoring the calm, reasoned stretches of their speeches.[10]

Joseph Boskin of Boston University defines a stereotype as "a standardized mental picture, or series of pictures, representing an oversimplified opinion or an uncritical judgment that is staggeringly tenacious in its hold over rational thinking." He says that once an image or stereotype of a group becomes implanted in popular lore, it becomes deeply embedded in people's minds and profoundly affects thoughts and actions. Furthermore, Boskin says, it is possible for a stereotype to grow in defiance of *all* evidence that it is incorrect.

Boskin states that ever since the 1600s, white Americans have envisioned the black person as either "a Sambo or a savage," and he says that of all the various stereotypes assigned to minority groups in this country over the centuries, this dual image of blacks has been the most long-lived and barbarous. "By labeling and perpetuating Sambo—meaning lazy, indolent, carefree, optimistic and intellectually limited—and the savage—a synonym for sexual prowess, dangerousness, and impulsiveness," Boskin writes, white society has rationalized its exploitation and oppression of blacks. He feels these stereotypes have contributed immeasurably to the racial conflict and violence of the past forty years and are a direct cause of continual underfinancing of welfare and affirmative action programs, urban policies, and social service programs.[11]

According to the conference participants and the empirical studies to be reported later, the media's representation of blacks strongly reinforced the cultural stereotype of American blacks, has helped prevent white acceptance of blacks as a normal part of American society, and thus has contributed to racial violence and oppression. This is a heavy onus to bear for a press that has prided itself on its devotion to neutrality and objectivity.

Doubtless a large part of journalists' damaging treatment of news about blacks was unconscious and is in itself a testimony to the tremendous power of a deeply embedded stereotype to influence a person's thoughts and behavior without the person's realizing it. In fact, it is possible to theorize that a popularly held stereotype may operate like the news framework Hartmann and Husband described; items that accord with the stereotype (or framework) may be much more likely to be run than those that do not. It seems increasingly obvious that in a society in which stereotypes are so deeply entrenched and which remains so effectively segregated that many citizens have no personal experience with blacks to counteract the stereotypes, objectivity in the media is not possible without, as Hugo Young says, a positive commitment to seek it.

Hartmann and Husband make the point that it is perfectly possible for racial prejudice and a strong commitment to egalitarian values to exist side by side within an individual and a society. This dual set of beliefs has led to several interesting examples of schizophrenia in the British press's treatment of race.

In their study of British press coverage of race in the 1960s, the authors found that on their editorial pages the newspapers deplored racial discrimination and oppression and expressed a concern for improved race relations, while in their news coverage of race they fostered the impression that colored immigrants were a threat and a problem and helped define the interracial situation in a way that promoted the development of attitudes of hostility rather than acceptance. By doing so, Hartmann and Husband note, the newspapers communicated a picture of the situation consistent with traditional British ethnocentrism and racism, despite "their affirmation of contrary values, and often in spite of their apparent intentions."[12]

Both Harold Evans and participants in a nine-nation seminar conducted by the Press Foundation of Asia in 1970 noted a similar schizophrenia based on examples of inflammatory news reports followed by righteous editorial sentiments. For example, the Press Foundation seminar reported on a Yorkshire newspaper that carried numerous news stories falsely suggesting that a Pakistani minority was responsible for an outbreak of smallpox. When the Pakistanis were then attacked, the newspaper condemned the attacks in an editorial. The seminar report stated, "It is recognized that editorial comment, however benign, does not necessarily compensate for the harm done by a misleading news report."[13] These examples illustrate how easily journalists' commitments to ideals of equality and justice can be subverted by the power of a deep-rooted prejudice to influence thoughts and actions in news coverage.

LACK OF PROBLEM COVERAGE

Another coverage deficiency noted by conference participants was the media's failure to portray to white readers what the Kerner Commission described as "the difficulties and frustrations of being a Negro in the United States." The socioeconomic data presented in the first chapter of this book present a bleak enough picture of the situation of many American blacks, and several decades ago, when the civil rights movement first gained momentum, the situation was still more appalling. Yet before the 1954 Supreme Court school desegregation decision, the plight of the American black was, as Dalsimer observed, just that—a plight, not a story.

Conference participants noted that before 1960 the communications media so effectively ignored the severe injustices and oppression experienced by American blacks that many white citizens were largely unaware of them. For example, Sylvan Meyer noted that during the 1950s the general impression southern newspapers gave their readers was that equality in education had been achieved. "I confess I was startled one day," Meyer wrote, "to hear a Negro educator read from the Georgia auditor's report figures of shocking inequity in my state's per pupil and per college allocations to Negro junior colleges as compared with white ones." He said the subject of the precise status of education for blacks had been forfeited by the press, as were disparities in a host of other services.[14]

Even in the coverage of the civil rights revolution many black problems, aside from segregation and racial violence in the South, were not explored in depth. National Urban League director Whitney Young said in the mid-1960s that "the press has failed to show that the Negro's grievances are real. To read the newspapers, you might think the Negro is reacting to some mild inconvenience."[15]

Perhaps the most telling measure of whites' ignorance of the problems facing black Americans was a 1967 Gallup poll which found that only one white American in one hundred thought blacks were being treated badly, and 75 percent thought blacks were treated the same as whites. The poll also found that the white public blamed ghetto uprisings on "outside agitators" and "Negroes demanding too much."[16] Such incredible ignorance of the realities of many black Americans' lives must be attributed partly to the media's failure to interpret the black experience for whites.

This particular omission, especially as it applied to ghetto problems, was scored by both the conference participants and the Kerner Commission. "The media report and write from the standpoint of a white man's world," the commission said. "The ills of the ghetto, the difficulties of life there, the Negro's burning sense of grievance, are seldom conveyed."[17]

In the book on the UCLA conference, Jack Lyle noted that because reporters rarely ventured into the black ghetto and rarely wrote of its problems, reporters were as ignorant of local ghetto conditions as their newspapers' readers were when the riots occurred.[18] Several other writers also have remarked that newspapers not only were as ignorant of ghetto conditions as their readers but also were just as surprised when the riots erupted. Yet after several years of riots, whites still were asking in bewilderment, "What do Negroes want?" The fact that the question had to be asked at all was a clear indication of the media's failure to present an accurate and comprehensive picture of the ghetto residents' situation.

When participants at the Columbia conference criticized superficial or inaccurate reporting of the ghetto by poorly informed journalists, media personnel answered that good reporting was more difficult in the ghetto than elsewhere because the ghetto had been neglected so long. They pointed out that the media had established no ground rules about what to cover and what to leave out, as they had in City Hall reporting, for instance. But participants pointed to the easily available nature of much relevant data on, for example, who owns ghetto properties, what proportions of cities' budgets go into ghettos, and how much money, equipment, and services are deployed in the ghetto in proportion to population.[19]

In a 1968 article, Ben Gilbert quoted a Federal Communications Commissioner who said, "A race riot is a form of communication. It is a man crying out, 'Listen to me, mister. There's something I've been trying to tell you and you're not listening.' "[20] Even if they had not been listening before, newspapers in many American cities did begin to listen *after* several major riots occurred in the mid-1960s. They sent reporters into the ghettos to try to discover the grievances of the residents, and their findings were printed in articles and even special sections. But some inner-city blacks felt this attention was suspect. As one Watts youth said after the 1965 riot, "The only time they care about us is when we start busting windows. All of a sudden everybody is running down here asking us what's wrong. Who they kidding?"[21]

A Los Angeles press critic expressed the same idea. Criticizing newspapers for being so slow to acknowledge white racism in our society, he said that the papers had failed to cover ghetto conditions extensively until after the Watts riot because they were afraid of offending their comfortable, middle-class readers who, "presumably, either didn't know about these conditions or, more likely, didn't object to them as long as they were not personally affected."[22]

Several writers have commented upon the media's tendency to ignore other social problems besides racial oppression or to cover them only cursorily. Caryl Rivers noted that when President Johnson declared a war on poverty, the news media suddenly discovered that poverty did in fact exist in America. "An unemployed coal miner in Appalachia woke up one morning to find reporters from the *New York Times*, AP, UPI and Reuters on his front step, wanting to interview him about poverty," Rivers wrote. "Today, that same coal miner may be just as poor, just as unemployed, but he is all alone. The reporters have gone."[23] John Hamilton says, "The 'invisible poor' that Michael Harrington discovered and wrote about in 1962 in *The Other America* have remained invisible to much of the American press and, therefore, to much of the American public."[24]

Perhaps the media truly do not care about the ghetto-trapped black, the poor, the hungry, the indigent elderly. Or perhaps they would cover these peoples' problems more thoroughly if media audiences and advertisers would accept such coverage. But are readers and viewers really so unwilling to be exposed to uncomfortable truths about social ills in America? Some of the readers and viewers are already deeply experiencing these ills; surely the rest of the public could endure learning about them.

It could be that media audiences are made uncomfortable by such coverage because they feel powerless to change the situations. But if the media not only illuminated the problems but also outlined suggested solutions, readers and viewers who were so inclined could perhaps see some methods of beginning to work toward change. In addition, the creation of informed public opinion could make possible the passage of necessary governmental measures to alleviate some of the problems.

LACK OF COVERAGE OF CAUSES

Closely related to the charges of media inattention to black problems was another criticism of coverage raised at the late 1960s conferences. This was the media's failure to cover adequately the conditions underlying the civil rights revolution and the causes of racial conflict. The media were praised for good coverage of the "Who? What? When? Where?" and "How?" of social protest but were faulted for giving scant attention to the "Why?" The Kerner Commission noted this failure of the media to fulfill their own traditional standards of good coverage when it stated that journalists generally had done a good job of covering the riots, sometimes risking their lives to do so, but also had failed to explain sufficiently the basic reasons for the disorders.[25]

Fisher and Lowenstein report that a charge frequently heard at the University of Missouri conference was that:

[T]he media have devoted too much time and space to "enumerating the wounded" and too little to describing the background problems of the Negro in America and the aims and goals of the Negro revolution. Speaker after speaker stressed the need to tell the whole story—to deal with de facto segregation, the difficulties encountered by Negroes in getting jobs, and the bias that lies beneath the surface.[26]

During the same conference, Dalsimer observed that "the news media often treat America's racial situation as though it were a plane disaster or a shipwreck. There is overemphasis on a one-shot event, while a half-century of rat infestation in tenements or a chronic unemployment rate is ignored."[27]

But this may have been the kind of coverage reporters were encouraged to provide. Media executives' preference for coverage that featured violence, and their disinterest in coverage of causes, is a theme mentioned by former network television reporter Paul Good in his book about covering the civil rights movement in the South in 1964. Good said he encountered this attitude among executives while covering America's racial story and had experienced it earlier when he was assigned to Latin America. He wrote that during his Latin American work, he received praises from his headquarters when he managed to get film of explosions and shootings. But if he suggested doing an analysis on the causes of the unrest, his superiors were not interested, he said.[28]

One result of coverage focused only on conflict is that the public is poorly informed about the causes of social upheaval. At the University of Missouri conference, Fanning said, "The media have tended to blur the issues by concentrating so much reportorial attention and energy on the number of wounded or killed, the number arrested, the number in the line of march." In their preoccupation with these kinds of facts, Fanning noted, the media failed to answer white readers' question: "What do they [black Americans] want?"[29]

Emphasizing conflict and ignoring the causes of protest also can cause readers to see protesters as threatening and unreasonably demanding, thus contributing to distrust and hostility between races and classes in the United States. In an article on the 1968 Poor People's March and other social protests, Blanchard wrote that the press tended to concentrate on the threatening aspects of protesters' behavior, to focus on violence and how many people got beaten and on gathering facts and quotes, rather than providing any background on the demonstrators' problems and grievances.

Because the press tended to cover social protests with such a superficial, "police-blotter" approach, Blanchard claimed, "The public is either uninformed or misinformed about the causes of domestic upheaval." This kind of coverage also, he said, presents the protesters' actions in such a threatening light that readers are frightened and alienated.[30]

Johnson, Sears, and McConahay, in their study of Los Angeles newspapers' coverage of blacks, suggest a chilling progression of events arising partly from the nature of the media's past coverage of blacks. They state that long-standing media inattention to blacks has contributed to white ignorance of and exploitation of blacks and indifference to their problems. The conflict-oriented coverage of the civil rights movement of the 1960s (perhaps coupled with the lack of attention to the causes of the protests) led to increased fear of blacks on the part of whites. This fear, exacerbated by the violence of the riots, was then used to justify further repression, the researchers indicate.[31] This analysis suggests that the media apparently cannot escape playing a central role in race relations, no matter how little they desire the part.

Failure to explain the causes of racial conflict is not a problem unique to the U.S. media. Hartmann and Husband write, in words that at first sound remarkably similar to the Kerner Commission's, that "the British news media have failed to report adequately on the underlying bases of racial conflict in this country, and in so doing have assisted in the scapegoating of coloured immigrants: in this their conflict framework has played a facilitating role."

The authors add that "it is vital that the news media should debate the background to conflict and not confine itself to monitoring the symptoms." They say, however, that a real commitment to such coverage may not occur. They explain that adequate discussion of the real reasons for unemployment and housing shortages in Britain would "remove the buffer of scapegoating and lay bare the actual social inequalities." Such discussion is not likely to be presented in the media, the authors say, "given the current pattern of ownership and control of the media and their close identification with those interests that gain more from social inequalities and the 'management' of conflicts rather than their removal."[32]

COVERAGE OF LOCAL SITUATIONS

Before the 1979 Soviet invasion of Afghanistan gave new meaning to the term, a word used by journalists to describe a certain kind of editorial stance was "Afghanistanism." The epithet described the practice of some newspaper editors of vigorously criticizing injustices in distant places that neither the editors nor their readers could do anything about, while ignoring injustices in their hometowns. During the civil rights movement, many news media—particularly northern ones—were criticized for falling into this same trap. The media tended to play up racial conflicts in other cities and parts of the country, critics said, while failing to cover racial injustices and tensions in their own areas.

Turner Catledge of the *New York Times* was quoted during the University of Missouri conference as saying at a 1963 editors' and publishers' conference, "We've had open season on the South here . . . for some time." He said that northern editors were "too much concerned with what's going on somewhere else and too little concerned with what's going on right at their own door." Integration was occurring very slowly in the South and was not wanted there, he said. But "is it wanted any more in Minnesota or New York?" he asked.[33]

During the Columbia conference, participants said that the media should strive "to overcome the fault of 'Afghanistanism' or 'Selmaism'—that is, failure to cover their own communities in depth." Noting that the best coverage of the Newark riots was done by the *Washington Post*, the participants said "there was no reason why the local media could not have done as well."[34]

The same point was raised at the UCLA conference by Jack Lyle, *Los Angeles Times* reporter Jack Jones, and southern editor Hodding Carter III. All commented that newspapers showed a tendency to cover racial flare-ups in other cities while ignoring as much as possible racial problems within their own areas.[35]

The problem with this kind of coverage is similar to that produced by the other kinds of coverage deficiencies already discussed. It presents white readers and viewers with a distorted picture of reality and conditions them to believe that they are in no way responsible for racism and injustice.

Johnson, Sears, and McConahay suggest that media concentration on southern racial segregation and violence had confused whites' understanding of racism in the North. "Northern whites cannot see 'white racism' in their own attitudes and behavior," the authors write, "because for the most part their actions do not even remotely resemble their image of the crude red-neck racism of the overt southern bigot. Thus they simply reject the notion that they contribute to racism." As supporting evidence, the authors refer to a 1968 CBS report of a poll that found only 31 percent of the whites sampled nationwide agreed with the Kerner Commission's charge blaming racial conflicts on "white racism."[36]

Paul Good said that the word "redneck" refers to ignorant and brutal people whom cultured southerners disdain in the same way that sophisticated New Yorkers look down on slum residents. What both the southerner and the New Yorker fail to realize, Good stated, is that their own indifference has helped to create the kinds of mentality and behavior they despise.[37]

This tendency to see the mote in another person's eye while not perceiving the beam in one's own is obviously a universal and deep-seated human failing. And it could even be theorized that media from outside a city may be able to cover that city's racial disturbances more objectively than the local media. But only the local media have a real stake in covering the conditions and causes underlying their city's racial problems and in illuminating the structure and strengths of the local black community. The *Atlanta Constitution* may send a reporter to cover Boston's school integration conflicts, but that reporter is not going to stay and try to present a comprehensive picture of the problems and the contributions of Boston's black citizens. Initiative to undertake that kind of in-depth coverage would have to come from the Boston media.

PREVIOUS EMPIRICAL STUDIES

Although the coverage deficiencies noted by the Kerner Commission, journalists, and others in the 1960s were based largely on subjective impressions and experience, their criticisms echoed the findings of earlier systematic analyses of coverage conducted by scholars. A score of empirical studies of newspaper coverage of blacks during the first half of this century indicated that the papers reflected white society's general indifference and sense of superiority toward blacks. The studies, two-thirds of which focused on periods between 1900 and 1932, showed that newspapers gave little space to news about blacks and heavily emphasized black crime in the news they did run.

For instance, a study by George Simpson of black news in the Philadelphia press between 1908 and 1932 found that coverage of blacks occupied less than 2 percent of the papers' total news space. He also found that news of crimes committed by blacks accounted for 52 to 74 percent of the total coverage given to blacks.[38]

A similar pattern of coverage was observed by Noel Gist in a study of sixty issues of seventeen major newspapers from various sections of the country during 1928–29. Gist found that 47 percent of the news run about blacks concerned antisocial behavior. Stating that the press distorted black news, emphasizing that which was bizarre and pathological in black life, Gist concluded, "Without a doubt any satisfactory explanation of the treatment of Negro news is to be found in the social attitudes that lie behind the press reports."[39]

The Chicago Commission on Race Relations, in a study published in 1922, condemned the Chicago press's presentation of news about blacks and said the 1919 Chicago race riots were due partly to antipathetic attitudes expressed by local newspapers.[40] Selma Warlick's 1931 study of news about blacks in the southern press found that the southern newspapers examined expressed no objections to the lynching of blacks, and Clifford Johnson's study of black news in Oregon newspapers between 1931 and 1945 indicated that the newspapers presented no information on black advances during this period and instead limited their coverage to black crime, entertainment figures, and sports personalities.[41]

In a study done in 1950, Florence Rebekah Beatty-Brown summarized the findings of the studies of black news coverage during the previous half-century by stating, "Evidence is multitudinous that newspapers all over the country, no matter what historical period is studied, discriminate against the Negro in the news."[42] One of the few positive findings in a study covering part of the first half of the century was reported by this same researcher in her study of coverage of blacks in 317 issues of the *St. Louis Post-Dispatch* between 1920 and 1950. Beatty-Brown found this newspaper to be unique among major American newspapers in its fairness and sympathetic attitude toward blacks, but she added that news about blacks appeared infrequently.[43]

Only a few empirical studies of newspaper coverage of blacks in the years between 1950 and 1970 have been done, and each of them illustrates some inadequacy of coverage. A content analysis of news about blacks in 180 issues of the *Wichita Eagle* during six months of 1968 led Robert Latta to the conclusion that the quantity and quality of the coverage were not adequate and that the newspaper failed to report on the serious economic, social, and political problems affecting the city's black population.[44]

Helen Louise Tatro studied local news coverage of blacks in forty-five issues of five Deep South newspapers between 1950 and 1970 and found no significant change in the frequency of items run about local blacks during this period. She also found that news about black crimes constituted 50 percent of the coverage in 1950 and 24 percent of the coverage in 1970.[45]

Johnson, Sears, and McConahay studied coverage of blacks in 215 issues of Los Angeles newspapers between 1892 and 1968 and found that less than 1 percent of the papers' available news space was devoted to blacks during most of the first 52 years of the period studied. The coverage increased to roughly 5 percent between 1964 and 1967, at the height of the civil rights movement, and peaked at 15 percent at the time of the 1965 Watts riot. The authors note that during the late 1950s and early 1960s, when the coverage rose to 5 percent, the black population of Los Angeles rose from about 12 to 15 percent of the city's total. They state that by giving scant attention to the black community except during racial conflicts, the press in Los Angeles was helping to perpetuate black invisibility and thus both embodied institutional racism and failed to combat the white public's ignorance about it.[46]

Several other studies of black-related news and editorial coverage between 1950 and 1970 suggest this same pattern of press inattention to black concerns. These works include Thomas Kelly's analysis of editorial attitudes toward racial problems in four Chicago newspapers between 1954 and 1968, Andrew Secrest's study of editorial leadership on racial matters by South Carolina newspapers during the same period, Roy Carter's study of the desegregation-related content of several North Carolina dailies after the 1954 Supreme Court decision, and Fred Fedler's study of two Minneapolis newspapers' coverage of twenty minority and twenty establishment groups.[47]

Thus, the empirical studies of press coverage of blacks during the first half of the century indicated that such coverage was scant and did not present an accurate picture of black life and concerns. Instead, in many cases the coverage was concentrated on crime news involving blacks and, to a lesser extent, on black sports and entertainment figures. These findings suggest that the press perpetuated stereotypes of the black criminal, athlete, and entertainer. The few empirical studies of coverage of blacks between 1950 and 1970 raised similar concerns but also noted a lack of attention to problems concerning blacks and a tendency to ignore black citizens and their situation except during times of racial conflict.

RESEARCH QUESTIONS

The research reported by scholars seems to substantiate the criticisms of press coverage of black Americans expressed by black citizens, journalists, and the Kerner Commission and indicates that coverage of blacks in the first fifty or sixty years of this century fell far short of the social responsibility standards outlined by the Commission on Freedom of the Press. What kinds of newspaper coverage of black citizens and of relations between the races might meet the standards expressed by these various groups?

First, it might be expected that newspapers would cover the same kinds of news about blacks as they do about whites, showing the ordinary life of the black community, as well as the unusual, and avoiding emphasis on stereotypical kinds of images. In addition, since black citizens, especially those who live in ghettos, experience severe obstacles in their attempts to enjoy equality of opportunity in America, newspapers could explain these problems to their readers and also point out suggested solutions.

Also, it might be expected that newspapers would explore and explain the causes of social protest and other confrontational activities involving blacks, instead of simply covering the conflicts as isolated events. In addition, papers could logically be expected to cover the problems of their local black communities, rather than focusing on conflicts in other locations. Finally, newspapers could be expected to eliminate from their coverage indications of bias, antipathy, and indifference toward black Americans.

The purpose of the study reported in the following chapters is twofold. First, an analysis of the coverage of American blacks in the four newspapers during selected years in the early 1950s and the 1960s was designed to ascertain whether these papers' performance exhibited the deficiencies suggested by both the empirical studies and the discussions of press coverage of blacks. In addition, a similar analysis of coverage during certain years of the 1970s attempted to determine whether the newspapers showed evidence of moving in the direction of the coverage improvements that were discussed during the late 1960s and suggested by the standards outlined by the Commission on Freedom of the Press.

Specific research questions to be answered by this study of the coverage of black Americans in the four newspapers were:

1. How much of the coverage presented a picture of the everyday life of black citizens and of blacks as a normal part of the total American society?

2. How much of the coverage was focused on stereotypical images of blacks?

3. How much of the coverage presented information about problems facing blacks?

4. In their coverage of the confrontational events of the civil rights struggle, how much explanation did the newspapers give to the causes underlying the events?

5. How much of the newspapers' coverage of racial conflicts and problems was devoted to such situations in their own cities?

6. Did the papers express, in their editorials and in other ways, indifference and antipathy toward blacks?

7. How did the newspapers' coverage in these areas change over the three time periods examined?

NOTES

1. Ben H. Bagdikian, "Editorial Responsibility in Times of Urban Disorder," in Daly, *The Media and the Cities*, p. 15.

2. *Conference on Mass Media and Race Relations*, pp. 9, 11.

3. Gilbert, "Race Coverage," p. 2.

4. *National Advisory Commission*, p. 383.

5. Ibid.

6. Schneider, *The Newsman and the Race Story*, p. ii.

7. *Race and the Press*, p. 23.

8. Hartmann and Husband, p. 145; emphasis original.

9. Bagdikian, p. 15.

10. *Conference on Mass Media and Race Relations*, p. 8.

11. Joseph Boskin, "Denials: The Media View of Dark Skins and the City," in Rubin, *Small Voices*, pp. 141–43.

12. Hartmann and Husband, pp. 145–46, 188.

13. *Race and the Press*, pp. 45, 56.

14. Meyer, "The Press and the Schools," p. 39.

15. Woody Klein, "The New Revolution: A Postscript," in Fisher and Lowenstein, *Race and the News Media*, p. 147.

16. Frank L. Stanley, Jr., "Race, Poverty and the Press," *ASNE Bulletin*, Sept. 1967, p. 2.

17. *National Advisory Commission*, p. 366.

18. Lyle, "Introduction," p. xiii.

19. *Conference on Mass Media and Race Relations*, p. 17.

20. Gilbert, "Race Coverage," p. 2.

21. Jack Jones, "Riot Leaves Sense of Helplessness," in *The View from Watts*, articles reprinted from the *Los Angeles Times*, 10–17 Oct. 1965 (Los Angeles: Los Angeles Times).

22. DeMott, p. 10.

23. Rivers, p. 56.

24. John A. Hamilton, "Telling It Like It Is," in Daly, *The Media and the Cities*, p. 53.

25. *National Advisory Commission*, p. 373.

26. Fisher and Lowenstein, p. 5.

27. Dalsimer, pp. 118–19.

28. Paul Good, *The Trouble I've Seen: White Journalist/Black Movement* (Washington, D.C.: Howard Univ. Press, 1975), p. 41.

29. Fanning, p. 111.

30. Blanchard, pp. 62–64.

31. Johnson, Sears, and McConahay, pp. 717–19.

32. Hartmann and Husband, p. 212.

33. George P. Hunt, "The Racial Crisis and the News Media: An Overview," in Fisher and Lowenstein, *Race and the News Media*, p. 15.

34. *Conference on Mass Media and Race Relations*, p. 14.

35. Lyle, "Introduction;" Jack Jones, "Comment by Jack Jones;" Hodding Carter III, "Comment by Hodding Carter III," in Lyle, *The Black American and the Press*, pp. ix, 34, 39.

36. Johnson, Sears, and McConahay, pp. 717–18.

37. Good, p. 54.

38. George E. Simpson, *The Negro in the Philadelphia Press* (Philadelphia: Univ. of Pennsylvania Press, 1936), pp. 6, 116.

39. Noel P. Gist, "The Negro in the Daily Press," *Social Forces* 10, no. 3 (March 1932), 406–11.

40. Ibid., p. 405.

41. Florence Rebekah Beatty-Brown, "The Negro as Portrayed by the St. Louis *Post-Dispatch* from 1920 to 1950," Diss. Univ. of Illinois at Urbana-Champaign, 1951, pp. 7, 10.

42. Ibid., p. 12.

43. Ibid., p. 294.

44. Robert L. Latta, "A Content Analysis of News of Black Americans as Presented by the Wichita *Eagle* and a Comparison with Empirical Data," *Journalism Abstracts* 9 (1971), 225.

45. Helen Louise Tatro, "Local News Coverage of Blacks in Five Deep South Newspapers, 1950 to 1970," *Journalism Abstracts* 10 (1972), 336.

46. Johnson, Sears, and McConahay, pp. 706–7, 718.

47. See Thomas James Kelly, "White Press/Black Man: An Analysis of the Editorial Opinion of the Four Chicago Daily Newspapers Toward the Race Problem, 1954–1968," Diss. Univ. of Illinois at Urbana-Champaign, 1971; Secrest; Roy E. Carter, "Segregation and the News: A Regional Content Study," *Journalism Quarterly* 34, no. 1 (Winter 1957), 3–18; and Fred Fedler, "The Media and Minority Groups: A Study of Adequacy of Access," *Journalism Quarterly* 50, no. 1 (Spring 1973), 109–17.

CHAPTER 5

Design of the Study

The newspaper study was designed so that information pertinent to all of the research questions posed in the preceding chapter could be obtained from an examination of the content of the four newspapers' coverage of American blacks during the thirty-year period being studied. For example, the papers' attention to stereotypical images of blacks, to the everyday-life activities of black citizens, and to black problems could be ascertained by noting the total column inches of coverage given to these kinds of topics.

It was possible to determine what proportion of the papers' coverage of protests was devoted to explaining the causes of the protests and how much of the coverage of racial conflicts and problems concerned local situations. Finally, information about whether the papers expressed white society's indifference toward blacks, as the Kerner Commission charged, was obtained from a study of editorials, the nature of the coverage of blacks, and the way the coverage was presented.

SAMPLE SELECTION

The newspapers chosen for the study—the *New York Times*, the *Boston Globe*, the *Atlanta Constitution*, and the *Chicago Tribune*—were selected for several reasons. First, it was thought that the criticisms voiced by the Kerner Commission and others of the American press's coverage of blacks and racial problems were aimed more at large-circulation, resource-rich metropolitan dailies than at smaller newspapers.

In addition, the newspapers selected are located in cities that experienced serious ghetto riots during the 1960s. Finally, the papers are published in cities that are located in four different areas of the country and that have a wide range of percentages of blacks in their populations, from 32 percent in Boston to 67 percent in Atlanta, according to the 1980 census.[1] A table showing the percentage of blacks in each city's population during all three time periods can be found in Appendix A.

Originally it was thought the *Los Angeles Times* should be included in the study, because it could represent coverage of blacks on the West Coast and because it is located in the city that experienced the first major urban riot of the 1960s. But the previously mentioned study by Johnson, Sears, and McConahay had already analyzed coverage of blacks by that newspaper through 1968, using coding categories roughly similar to those planned for this project. The pertinent findings of their study will be reported in the next chapter.

It should be noted that both the *New York Times* and the *Atlanta Constitution* may be in a sense atypical in their coverage of news concerning black Americans. Because the *Times* strongly emphasizes coverage of the theater, performing arts, and politics, one might expect to find items about black artists and political figures appearing more often in this newspaper than in most other papers. The *Constitution* has a record of extensive coverage of cultural, social, and educational events in Atlanta and the surrounding area, and this also might produce more frequent coverage of black Americans.

An additional fact worth noting is that blacks in all four cities represented by newspapers in this study have access to black newspapers from which to obtain more complete information about black concerns than can be found in the larger-circulation, white-owned papers. In New York and Chicago, the *Amsterdam News* and *Chicago Defender* have served black readers since early in the twentieth century, and black newspapers established in the 1960s cover concerns of blacks in Atlanta and Boston.

The first portion of this study was designed to sample coverage of blacks for several years before the civil rights revolution gained momentum, since the events of the movement would naturally have produced more press attention to blacks than had been the norm for the previous period. Because the civil rights movement is considered to have begun with the Supreme Court's school desegregation decision in 1954 and the Montgomery bus boycott of 1955–56, the four-year period of 1950 through 1953 was chosen for study.

The next portion of the project was an examination of coverage of blacks after the civil rights struggle was well underway, so the six years of 1963 through 1968 were chosen for study. This time period begins with the March on Washington led by Dr. Martin Luther King and includes the passage of the 1964 Civil Rights Act, civil rights demonstrations and strong white resistance to federally ordered integration in the South, ghetto riots, the assassination of Dr. King, and the increasing shift of political protest action and press attention to the war in Viet Nam.

The focus of the final portion of the project was a study of how the newspapers covered blacks after the confrontational events of the civil rights revolution had ceased and after the papers had had time to begin implementing some of the improved coverage strategies discussed during the 1960s. Accordingly, the years 1972 through 1980 were chosen for study.

The newspapers were drawn randomly from a stratified sample of months, weeks of the months, and days of the week. A sample of three issues a year for the four-year period to be studied in the 1950s was drawn, making a total of twelve issues for each of the four newspapers. Because some of the sample issues were unavailable, the resulting total sample for that period was forty-five.

For the six-year period to be examined in the 1960s, a sample of four issues a year was drawn, for a total of twenty-four issues for each of the four newspapers. Since some of the issues of the *Chicago Tribune* were not available, the total sample for this period was eighty-four issues.

Because the study of coverage of blacks during the 1970s was the focus of this project, it was decided to sample more issues per year for this period. Also, since none of the years between 1972 and 1980 was unusually significant nor unimportant in terms of black-related news events, it was decided that samples from every other year from this period would provide a satisfactory overview of the coverage during this time. Accordingly, a sample of six issues a year for the five even-numbered years between 1972 and 1980 was drawn, for a total of thirty issues per newspaper. Inaccessibility of some issues of the *Tribune* resulted in a total sample of 116 issues for the 1970s. The sample size total for all three periods was 245 issues.

CODING INSTRUMENT

An instrument for coding the content into categories was devised after a study of the coverage itself.[2] Coverage of black Americans in several issues of each newspaper for each of the three time periods was analyzed, and a coding instrument was drawn up that provided as specifically as possible for all the different kinds of items found.

The recording unit for the project was any newspaper item—news or feature story, editorial or opinion column, letter to the editor, photo, or cartoon—that concerned American blacks or events involving blacks or directly affecting them, such as passage of civil rights legislation. All items in each sample issue, except for those in the sports sections, were scanned, and any pertinent items were measured in column inches and assigned to the appropriate subcategory on the basis of the item's topic. A total of 1,241 items was coded.

In cases where an item might be assigned to several different categories, its assignment was determined by the nature of the topic that received the greatest amount of space within the item. If an item covered various topics, only some of which concerned blacks, only those sections of the item referring to blacks were measured. If 75 percent or more of the article concerned blacks, the item's headline was measured and included. Since the column widths of the stories varied from one paper to another and within the papers themselves over the time period studied, all column-inch measurements were converted to a column 2.25 inches wide in order to facilitate comparisons among the individual newspapers and across time.

The instrument used in coding the content included sixteen subcategories that were grouped into four main categories. The first of these main categories was stereotypical coverage and included the subcategories of antisocial actions—primarily crimes committed by blacks—and entertainment figures. This category was labeled stereotypical because the review of the empirical studies had indicated that news about black crime and entertainment and sports figures comprised the bulk of coverage given to blacks in many American newspapers studied prior to the 1960s.

The sports sections of the newspapers were not coded in this study because the emphasis of the project was on general news coverage of American blacks. In cases where items about black sports figures were encountered in the other sections of the papers, they were coded into the stereotypical category.

· The second main category was everyday life, and this included subcategories of news that showed blacks as part of the normal life of the community. Such subcategories included community activities, individual achievements, political activities, local officeholders at work, disasters, and interracial violence. This main category was designed to include all items that portrayed the activities of the black community and that showed black citizens within the context of the total American society—the kinds of coverage that the press was criticized for providing in insufficient amounts during the 1960s and earlier. Items directly related to the civil rights struggle were not included in this section but were coded into the next main category.

The third main category, civil rights, included subcategories of news concerned with the black struggle for equality, such as black protests, riots, white resistance to integration, civil rights gains, other civil rights–related news, and white leaders calling for integration. Some subcategories within this section provided opportunity for study of the way the newspapers approached coverage of the civil rights struggle.

For example, the literature had suggested that newspapers focused on the conflict aspects of civil rights protests and provided scant explanation of the causes of the events. In order to test out this assertion, provision was made on the coding instrument for recording the amount of space given to explanation of causes in each story on black protest. Also, since several sources in the literature had suggested that the press tended to play up racial conflicts and problems in other cities while downplaying those in their own, the coding instrument made provision for the researcher to enter the geographic location of each conflict-oriented civil rights event and problem story.

The final main category of the coding instrument, minority life, included the subcategories black problems and housing programs. This main category was devised to include coverage that was not directly civil rights–related but which pertained to blacks' position as a minority group within American society. The black problems subcategory provided a picture of press attention to the problems faced by black citizens during the periods studied. The housing program subcategory included items about urban renewal and other housing programs in black inner-city neighborhoods. The coding instrument also required the coder to enter in narrative form the subject of each problem story and the dominant assertions of any editorials about blacks, the civil rights struggle, and integration.

Although the column-inch totals in the various coverage categories and subcategories can answer many of the research questions posed earlier, they cannot adequately show whether the newspapers did, as the Kerner Commission charged, betray the biases and indifference of white America. The presence of bias in news coverage or headline treatment, the attitudes expressed in editorials, and the newspapers' general approach to coverage of blacks all are examples of subjects that must be described in narrative form; they do not lend themselves to description by numbers.

Therefore, an important aspect of this study, and the method to be used to answer at least one of the research questions, was qualitative analysis of the study's findings. Notes were taken on the assertions made in editorials, on display of the items, and on other information which seemed to provide clues to the newspaper managements' general attitude toward black Americans, their problems, and their struggle for equality. An attempt was made to flesh out the coverage tabulations with narrative description of these observations.

A pilot test of the coding instrument was made by coding several issues of each newspaper for each of the time periods to be studied. A measurement of the total available news space in each issue sampled was sought for discussion purposes, and the pilot test revealed that hand measuring the news hole—or available news space—of each issue required more time than coding the relevant items in the issue. For this reason it was decided to estimate each newspaper's news space rather than hand measure it.

The estimate was based on annual reports published in *Editor & Publisher* in 1959 and 1979 of the ratio of news versus advertising run in the four newspapers used in this study.[3] Other researchers who have used this method report an error of 2 percent or less when such estimates are compared with the results of hand measuring the space.[4]

In order to check coding reliability, two persons not involved in the study independently coded four sample issues each. The issues included a total of at least twenty-two items. Intercoder reliability was estimated on the basis of the coders' decisions about the number of items referring to blacks in each issue and the subcategories to which the items were assigned. The formula devised by Holsti, which divides agreed-upon subcategory assignments by the number of assignments made, was used.[5] Intercoder reliability was 0.86.

NOTES

1. U.S. Department of Commerce, Bureau of the Census, *1980 Census of Population and Housing, Final Population and Housing Unit Count* (Washington, D.C.: Government Printing Office, 1981), and *1980 Census of Population*, vol. 1, *Characteristics of the Population*, ch. C, *General Social and Economic Characteristics*, pt. 23, *Massachusetts* (Washington, D.C.: Government Printing Office, 1983).

2. The complete coding instrument and instructions may be found in the author's *Coverage of Black Americans in Four Metropolitan Newspapers Between 1950 and 1980*, obtainable on microfilm from the Kent State University Library, Kent, Ohio 44242.

3. During the 20 years between 1958 and 1978 this ratio changed no more than 0.03 in each of the newspapers except the *Atlanta Constitution*, where the percentage of news run dropped almost 0.09 in that same period. Thus, it seemed safe, for all the papers except the *Constitution*, to use the 1958 figures to estimate the papers' percentage of news hole in the early 1950s; the figure used for the *Constitution* for the early 1950s is less likely to be accurate than that used for the other papers. Even if a figure a few percentage points higher or lower were used to estimate the *Constitution*'s news hole in the early 1950s, however, the result would still show that this newspaper ran a higher proportion of news about blacks than the other newspapers did.

4. Robert L. Jones and Roy E. Carter, Jr., "Some Procedures for Estimating 'News Hole' in Content Analysis," *Public Opinion Quarterly* 23, no. 3 (Fall 1959), 399–403.

5. Richard W. Budd, Robert K. Thorp, and Lewis Donohew, *Content Analysis of Communications* (New York: Macmillan, 1967), p. 68.

CHAPTER 6

Findings of the Study

This study indicates that during the early 1950s the four newspapers provided very little coverage of black Americans, both in column inches and as a percentage of their available news space. This finding provides some support for the statements made by journalists and the Kerner Commission that prior to 1954 many American newspapers tended to ignore blacks. It also reflects the findings of other researchers who discovered that in several major cities, during the first half of the century, newspapers devoted only 1 to 2 percent of their available news hole to coverage of blacks.[1] As Figure 1 indicates, during the early 1950s, the *Atlanta Constitution* was the only newspaper of the four studied whose coverage of black citizens accounted for as much as 1 percent of total available news space.

As expected, coverage of blacks increased sharply during the 1960s in the newspapers studied because of the abundance of newsworthy civil rights activities that occurred at this time. The study by Johnson, Sears, and McConahay, the only empirical study besides this one that compared newspaper coverage of blacks before and during the civil rights movement as a percentage of total available news space, found that news about blacks in the *Los Angeles Times* rose from less than 1 percent of the paper's news hole in the early 1950s to 5 percent in the mid-1960s and 7 percent by 1968.[2] Figure 1 shows that while the newspapers studied in this project considerably increased their coverage of black Americans during the 1960s, in none of the papers did this coverage account for more than 4 percent of the total news hole.

Because both the confrontational activities of the civil rights struggle and the inner-city riots had largely ceased by 1972, it was ex-

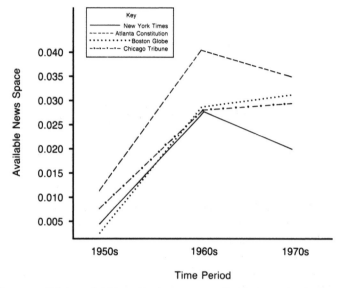

Source: Total available news space was estimated on the basis of annual reports of each newspaper's ratio of advertising to news content as published in "Quantitative Analysis of the Content of Morning, Evening, and Sunday Newspapers for the Year 1958," _Editor & Publisher_, 21 March 1959, p.66, and "Ad-News Ratio for 238 Dailies in 83 Markets," _Editor & Publisher_, 14 April 1979, p.12.

Figure 1. Estimated percentage of news hole devoted to coverage of blacks in four newspapers during three time periods (for exact column inch figures for available news space see Appendix B)

pected that each newspaper's coverage of blacks would show a sharp decline in the 1970s and would perhaps fall back to a level approaching the 1950s coverage. This was not the case, however. Perhaps the most surprising finding of the study was that during the 1970s the coverage in two of the papers *increased* from the previous level, and in the other two newspapers the decline was slight. In fact, in one of the two papers in which the decline was small, the coverage increased in terms of column inches, although it decreased as a percentage of available news space.

Figure 1 shows that in the 1970s coverage of blacks increased in both the *Boston Globe* and the *Chicago Tribune*, as a percentage of the

Table 1
Mean Number of Column Inches Per Issue and Percentage of Coverage of Black Americans By Main Categories of Coverage in Four Newspapers During Three Time Periods

Main category of coverage	Time Period:	1950s				1960s				1970s			
	Newspaper:	NYT	AC	BG	CT	NYT	AC	BG	CT	NYT	AC	BG	CT
Stereotypical		1.83 (10%)	4.83 (22%)		15.00 (47%)	6.92 (5%)	4.28 (6%)	2.80 (4%)	16.89 (17%)	13.31 (14%)	15.56 (18%)	7.31 (8%)	12.08 (15%)
Everyday Life		3.25 (18%)	7.92 (35%)	0.78 (17%)	8.42 (26%)	27.92 (19%)	10.27 (14%)	7.50 (11%)	15.04 (15%)	47.14 (49%)	48.71 (55%)	25.92 (30%)	43.03 (54%)
Civil Rights - Related		10.08 (56%)	8.83 (40%)	3.77 (84%)	4.33 (14%)	109.21 (74%)	52.17 (69%)	51.69 (79%)	70.66 (69%)	21.98 (23%)	15.07 (17%)	50.42 (58%)	14.72 (18%)
Minority Life		3.16 (17%)	1.00 (4%)		4.25 (13%)	3.58 (2%)	9.04 (12%)	4.17 (6%)		14.55 (15%)	9.16 (10%)	3.19 (3%)	10.00 (13%)
Total		18.33 (100%)	22.58 (100%)	4.55 (100%)	32.00 (100%)	147.63 (100%)	75.77 (100%)	66.14 (100%)	102.59 (100%)	96.98 (100%)	88.48 (100%)	86.85 (100%)	79.83 (100%)

papers' news hole, over what it had been in the 1960s. Even in the other two papers, where coverage decreased as a percentage of available news space from what it had been in the 1960s, it remained closer to its 1960s than its 1950s level.

In addition, Table 1 shows that one of these papers, the *Atlanta Constitution*, ran *more* column inches of coverage of blacks in the 1970s than it did in the 1960s, even though this represented a smaller percentage of the paper's news hole than it had in the previous period. Also during the 1970s, the other paper, the *New York Times*, ran more column inches of coverage of blacks in every subcategory and main category, except for civil rights, than it had in the 1960s.

This unexpected finding of continuing newspaper attention to news about American blacks during the 1970s suggests that the events of the 1960s—the activities of the civil rights revolution, the legislative progress toward black equality, the ghetto riots, and perhaps also the journalists' own discussions of the nature of their coverage of black Americans—produced among the managements of the newspapers studied an increased awareness of blacks and, perhaps, a desire to cover them more extensively and realistically than they had in the past.

The continued attention to blacks among the newspapers examined may also have resulted partly from an increased visibility and participation of black citizens in the everyday life of American society. Many more blacks were elected to Congress, to state legislatures, as mayors, and to other public offices during the 1970s than had held office in the two previous periods studied. Also, in the 1970s the papers seemed to find more black professional persons and business figures to cover than they had in the 1960s, perhaps partly because of affirmative action programs inspired by the civil rights movement.

EVERYDAY-LIFE AND STEREOTYPICAL COVERAGE

Andrew Secrest, discussing coverage of black citizens in South Carolina newspapers in the mid-1950s, wrote that the black man was "just as thoroughly segregated in the pages of South Carolina newspapers as he was in public schools or private cemeteries." Few pictures of blacks appeared, Secrest stated, and few articles were run about the black community's schools, civic organizations, business leaders, or social and professional activities. He noted that the black man seldom appeared in the papers' news columns except as a criminal or as a spokesman for a racial reform group—which to some readers amounted to the same thing, Secrest observed.[3]

Although Secrest was referring to South Carolina newspapers, by some measures his words could apply to the way the newspapers studied in this project covered the black American during the early 1950s. In the papers examined from this period, no stories or pictures about blacks were found on any of the newspapers' society, financial, or obituary papers, except in the *Atlanta Constitution*, where news of deaths of blacks was presented in a separate section of the obit page labeled "Colored." Blacks were rarely shown in pictures, in the stories studied, and were nearly always identified in stories as "Negro." The papers did not seem to show blacks as part of the ordinary life of the community.

The quantitative measure of the papers' coverage during this period, however, presents a slightly different picture. As Table 1 shows, the *Atlanta Constitution* and, to a smaller extent, the *Chicago Tribune*, devoted a considerable percentage of their total coverage of blacks to everyday-life activities.

The Kerner Commission and the journalists who discussed media coverage of blacks in the 1960s, as well as the scholarly studies mentioned earlier, suggested that newspapers had traditionally focused on stereotypical coverage of black entertainers and crimes committed by blacks. This claim is partially supported by the findings shown in the 1950s column of Table 1.

The two papers which provided the greatest amount of coverage of blacks and the greatest attention to everyday-life coverage during this period—the *Atlanta Constitution* and the *Chicago Tribune*—also concentrated heavily on stereotypical coverage of blacks. The *Tribune* especially displayed an inordinate preoccupation with this kind of coverage, giving it 47 percent of the paper's total coverage of blacks in the issues sampled.

In the cases of these two papers, earlier researchers' claims about media emphasis on the stereotype of the black criminal seem to be borne out. Coverage of crimes committed by blacks accounted for 20 percent of the *Constitution*'s 22 percent of stereotypical coverage and 41 percent of the *Tribune*'s 47 percent of stereotypical coverage, as Tables 5 and 7 in the next chapter will show.

The *Constitution*'s general attention to news about blacks is not surprising, since blacks constituted 37 percent of Atlanta's population at this time. However, the *Tribune* devoted even more space to coverage of blacks than the *Constitution* did—and emphasized black crime twice as heavily—even though blacks represented only 14 percent of Chicago's population then. The explanation for this disproportionate emphasis may arise from Chicago's having experienced a considerable influx of black emigrants from the South after World War II. The *Tribune* seems to have reacted to these arrivals the way Hartmann and Husband say the British press tended to respond to the large numbers of Asian and African immigrants into Britain during the 1950s and 1960s—with coverage that portrayed the newcomers as a threat and a problem.

The Johnson, Sears, and McConahay study showed a similar emphasis on stereotypical coverage. Although blacks represented only about 8 percent of the total population of Los Angeles in 1950 and had climbed to about 13 percent in 1960, stereotypical coverage of blacks in the *Los Angeles Times* was 17 percent in the 1940 to 1954 period, 19 percent between 1954 and 1965, and 17 percent between 1965 and 1966.[4]

It was expected that the largest proportion of the increased coverage of black Americans in the 1960s would be found in the civil rights–related category, and this expectation was supported in the data shown in the 1960s column of Table 1. Civil rights–related activities accounted for 69 percent to 79 percent of the total coverage of blacks during this period in each paper studied. The papers' attention to stereotypical and everyday-life activities in the 1960s dropped as a percentage of total coverage of blacks but increased in column inches in nearly all the papers.

Civil rights–related coverage, including items about interracial violence, accounted for 48 percent of the *Los Angeles Times*' coverage of blacks between 1940 and 1954, according to Johnson, Sears, and McConahay. This figure rose to 56 percent between 1954 and 1965, and to 68 percent between 1965 and 1966. During these same time periods the proportions of everyday-life coverage of blacks in the *Los Angeles Times* and the *Herald-Examiner* were only 7 percent, 5 percent, and 3 percent.[5]

Although the newspapers studied in this project gave more inches of coverage to blacks during the 1960s, by some indicators they continued to pay little attention to black citizens. News and photos of blacks remained absent from the society and financial sections of all four newspapers, except for three issues out of the eighty-four sampled from this period. Blacks also remained absent from the obituary pages, except for the "Colored" section of the *Constitution*'s obituary pages and one story in the *New York Times*. By 1968, however, all the papers had dropped the designation "Negro" from stories where race was not pertinent, and the "Colored" label disappeared from the *Constitution*'s obituary pages.

These findings lend support to the Kerner Commission's and journalists' concern in the 1960s that the press was failing to present news about the black community and to present blacks in the context of the total society. In addition, the findings raise the possibility that the managements of the newspapers studied were only slowly coming to view black Americans as members of society worth covering in their own right, separate from the phenomenon of the civil rights movement.

The papers apparently remained more aware of black citizens during the 1970s. Table 1 shows that the most evident change in the coverage distribution during the 1970s was a definite increase in each paper's attention to news about everyday-life activities of blacks and a corresponding decrease in attention to civil rights–related topics. But each paper except for the *Chicago Tribune*—a noteworthy exception—also increased its stereotypical coverage, both in column inches and as a percentage of total coverage, during this period.

The content of the coverage during the 1970s provides several examples of changes in the way the papers covered blacks and showed them as part of the normal life of the community. These changes seem to represent definite progress over the way the papers covered blacks in the early 1950s, because the 1970s coverage presented a more representative picture of blacks within American society.

For instance, the *New York Times* ran stories about black businesses or businessmen three times in the issues studied, its society pages included several photos of black models showing fashions, and obituaries of prominent blacks appeared four times. Engagement photos of black women appeared on the society pages of the *Atlanta Constitution* several times in the issues studied, and a black model was pictured in the *Boston Globe*'s society pages.

The *Chicago Tribune* featured a black businessman once in its financial pages in the issues coded and ran a photo of a black woman twice in its society pages. In addition, the paper had its own black columnist during the latter part of the 1970s period studied. Each of the four papers ran at least one obituary of a well-known black.

In the 1970s issues sampled, all the newspapers except for the *Tribune* ran several human interest features each about individual local blacks who were in some way interesting or outstanding. These were the first feature stories found about nonprominent black Americans—none were found in any of the 129 issues coded from the 1950s and 1960s. During these two earlier periods the only times features on blacks were found were upon the occasion of a black person's appointment or election to a prominent position or a well-known black's retirement or death.

The findings also suggest that a new stereotype—in the sense of a conventional mental image—of blacks may have begun to emerge in the papers' coverage in the 1970s. If the press stereotype of blacks in the 1950s and earlier was that of the criminal, entertainer, and athlete, in the 1960s the stereotype was the black demonstrator; coverage of black protests accounted for between 9 and 24 percent of the papers' total coverage of blacks in that period, as Tables 4 through 7 will show, and news involving black protesters also appeared frequently in other subcategories.

But in the 1970s the stereotype may well have been the black politician. The papers studied devoted between 8 and 20 percent of their total coverage of blacks in this period to items about political activities and local officeholders (see Tables 4 through 7).

It is important to note that this focus on the black politician and, earlier, on the black protester, may have been simply a reflection of reality, where the earlier emphasis on black criminals represented a distortion of reality. However, it would seem that *any* stereotype in news coverage is dangerous, because it may influence journalists to cover news that conforms to the stereotype and to ignore perhaps equally important items that contradict it.

COVERAGE OF BLACK PROBLEMS

One of the assumptions underlying this project was that during the thirty-year period under study American blacks were experiencing severe problems that the press, under the expectations of the

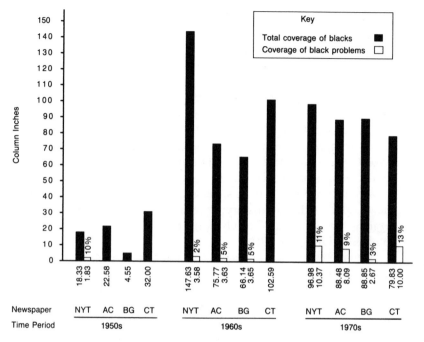

Figure 2. Mean number of column inches per issue of coverage of black problems as percentage of total coverage of blacks in four newspapers during three time periods

social responsibility theory, should have covered. The empirical literature had suggested, and the journalists and Kerner Commission had charged, that during the 1950s and even at the height of the civil rights movement the press had not often provided readers with information about the problems facing blacks.

The information presented in Figure 2 partially supports this contention. The figure also illustrates clearly the considerable changes in the papers' average column inches per issue of coverage of blacks during the period studied. In the 1950s issues sampled only the *New York Times* provided any information about black problems; it ran one wire service story on housing discrimination in Washington, D.C.

In the 1960s the newspapers' attention to problems experienced by blacks did increase; the *Atlanta Constitution* and *Boston Globe* joined the *New York Times* in providing some coverage in this area, while the *Chicago Tribune* continued to provide no information about black problems in the issues sampled.

However, the amount of coverage devoted to this topic seems rather small in light of the newsworthiness of the civil rights story at this time. During the University of Missouri conference, Samuel Dalsimer said that by the mid-1960s the media realized that "racial issues comprised America's most urgent domestic problem," and Woody Klein said that by 1967 all the media considered civil rights a top-running story which had been good copy in every American newsroom since 1963.[6] If Dalsimer and Klein were correct about the news value of the racial story, it seems surprising that the papers examined ran such a relatively small amount of coverage of black problems during the 1960s.

A common practice among the newspapers studied was, when covering a major running story, to assign reporters to write sidebar stories on peripheral aspects of the phenomenon and the background of the situation. One might have expected that during the 1960s the papers examined would have devoted considerable attention to explaining to their readers the causes—the problems facing blacks—behind the civil rights movement. That they did not devote more attention to black problems than they did could be interpreted as evidence that they were either ignorant of or indifferent to the black American's situation and grievances.

Surprisingly, all of the papers studied except the *Boston Globe* devoted much more space, in both column inches and as a proportion of their total coverage of blacks, to black problems during the 1970s than they did in the 1960s issues coded. This increase perhaps shows that the newspapers' managements had become sensitized to the situation of American blacks and were beginning to present a picture of some aspects of this situation to their readers. It is encouraging that they were doing so even though the confrontational events of the civil rights movement had ceased and the racial story was thus less newsworthy in the traditional sense. The topics covered in the black problem stories coded can be found in Appendix C.

Less encouraging is the finding, shown in Figure 3, that during the 1970s the papers devoted much less attention to the problems of local blacks than they had in the 1960s. The stories on local prob-

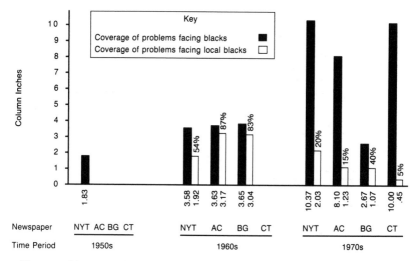

Figure 3. Mean number of column inches per issue of coverage of problems of local blacks as percentage of total coverage of black problems in four newspapers during three time periods

lems run during the earlier period were often sidebars to current news stories or installments in a series about local situations, and most of them were written by local reporters. Conversely, although many more stories on black problems were run during the 1970s than during the 1960s, most of these were wire and news service stories and syndicated columns about the problems of blacks across the nation.

The papers ran many stories about unemployment and health problems of blacks nationwide and about discrimination against blacks in this country's criminal justice system, but they did not use their own reporters to localize these stories and explore these situations among blacks in their circulation areas. In a sense, a form of "Afghanistanism" seemed to continue to operate; the papers' managements seemed willing to remind readers that blacks continued to experience oppression in American society, but they avoided troubling readers by failing to cover instances of black suffering uncomfortably close to home.

Another finding with negative implications was that the papers studied still were apparently unwilling to come to grips with the

Table 2

Number of Black Problem Stories Run in Issues Coded of Four Newspapers in Three Time Periods, Compared to Ghetto Residents' Grievances as Reported by the Kerner Commission[a]

Problems	Number of stories run		
Time Period:	1950s	1960s	1970s
A. REPORTED BY KERNER COMMISSION			
First level of intensity[b]			
Police practices			1
Unemployment, underemployment		2	6
Inadequate housing			
Second level of intensity			
Inadequate education			
Poor recreation facilities, programs			
Third level of intensity			
Ineffectiveness of political structure, grievance mechanisms			
Disrespectful white attitudes			
Discrimination in administration of justice		3	2
Inadequacy of federal programs, municipal services		2	1
Discriminatory consumer, credit practices			
Inadequate welfare programs		1	2
B. NOT REPORTED BY THE KERNER COMMISSION			
Poverty, hunger		1	2
Environmental problems in ghetto		1	1
Ghetto crime			3
Health problems			7
Discrimination in housing	1	1	1
White hatred, indifference			5
Problems of black professional persons			2

[a] The Kerner Commission surveyed ghetto residents in various riot cities in 1967 concerning the residents' belief about the grievances that had caused the riots (National Advisory Commission, p. 143). Numerous similarities can be observed between the findings of the commission's survey and those of the Detroit Free Press's survey of black ghetto residents in that city several weeks after the 1967 riot there and again a year later. The Free Press survey showed that the respondents presented the following grievances as the major causes of the riot: police brutality, poor housing, poverty, lack of jobs, overcrowded living conditions, failure of parents to control children, dirty neighborhoods, teenagers, too much drinking, broken political promises (Philip Meyer, Return to 12th Street: A Follow-up Survey of Attitudes of Detroit Negroes, October, 1968 [Detroit: Detroit Free Press, 1968], p. 8).

[b] The Kerner Commission reported the grievances in levels of related intensity to the ghetto residents surveyed.

phenomenon of the black ghetto and the situation of the people who live there. As Table 2 indicates, the problems the newspapers covered in the 1970s were not, in most cases, the ones that concerned ghetto residents most deeply in the late 1960s. The table shows which problems were covered as compared to a list of grievances compiled during a Kerner Commission survey of black ghetto residents in riot cities during 1967. The survey listed the problems in order of their intensity for black respondents. As the coverage matrix presented in Table 2 shows, few of the grievances presented as most serious by the ghetto residents surveyed were explored by the newspapers during any of the three periods studied.

Yet these problems continue to merit media attention. The 1981 Gannett News Service special report on the situation of the American black echoed a warning found in several editorials coded from the 1970s. "There is widespread agreement among urban experts that little has changed in America's cities in the past decade," the report stated, "except that in some the quality of life has declined even further, central cities have become blacker and poorer, and those stuck there have fewer options to escape." The report noted that the same ghetto social and economic conditions that the Kerner Commission found had persisted through 1981 and remained largely unresolved.[7]

This information suggests that newspapers should have been, in the 1970s, exploring and presenting to readers information on the situations that gave rise to the grievances listed in Table 2 and on the existence of such conditions in their own cities. If the media ignore these problems, a replay of the events of the 1960s seems inevitable for the future: the ghettos will again explode, the public and the media will once more be shocked and stunned, and the media will again be castigated for failing to alert the public to severe social problems until violence has erupted.

It seems worthwhile to include here a narrative description of some of the impressions obtained from coding the coverage of problems during the three time periods. This description can provide further information about the newspapers' attention to black problems and can also, indirectly, help answer the question of whether the newspapers did reflect white society's indifference and antipathy toward blacks.

Although only one story on the problems facing blacks was found in the forty-five issues coded from the 1950s, some short news stories coded under other subcategories provide a glimpse of the kinds of discrimination facing blacks at this time. For example, one article concerned University of North Carolina students protesting the university administration's refusal to allow six black law students to sit in the white section at football games. A 1952 *New York Times* story told of the NAACP demanding a first-degree murder indictment against an off-duty white policeman who allegedly shot two black men outside a bar in White Plains *because he objected to their presence in the bar*. He had been charged with second-degree murder.

Ironically, in 1980 the same newspaper reported blacks protesting the fact that five Miami policemen accused of beating a black insurance salesman to death had been charged only with manslaughter. The men's acquittal set off the Miami riots, and a *Times* editorial commented that, despite all the efforts of the past decades, "precious little progress" had been made in police relations with blacks.

The *Constitution* reported in 1951 that a Georgia lawyer was seeking a temporary injunction prohibiting the sheriff from beating a black prisoner. Perhaps the most poignant item of all was a sentence in a story about a black man who had qualified for the governor's race in Louisiana in the early 1950s. The reporter observed simply, "Negroes have been voting in Louisiana for years." The newspapers' failure to cover any of these types of situations in depth in the issues coded from the 1950s lends credence to the Kerner Commission's charge that the press reflected white society's indifference toward black Americans.

A little more attention to black problems was found in the issues coded from the 1960s, although the amount of coverage was still surprisingly small considering the racial furor then occurring. A total of only eleven problem stories was found in the eighty-four issues coded. Even more noteworthy, however, was the way the papers' *news* coverage gave readers a vivid picture of just one aspect of the problems facing American blacks—the white southerner's implacable determination to maintain a segregated way of life.

Much of the news coverage showed southern public schools, restaurants, and amusement parks closing to avoid the necessity of integration, a black musician being arrested for trying to check into a Louisiana motel, a black woman being arrested for standing in a "white women only" voting line, and Governor Wallace publicly telling the Alabama legislature to find ways to prevent blacks from being elected to local public office. And this was only the nonviolent resistance portrayed.

Also presented were stories of civil rights workers in the South being murdered by snipers, peaceful civil rights demonstrators being beaten while white police stood by watching—or did the beating themselves, and children being killed by bombs planted in black churches. Although other problems experienced by blacks were touched upon in the issues coded for this period, the clearest picture presented of the difficulties facing blacks was of the segregation of public facilities and disenfranchisement in the South and white southerners' determination to keep things that way. Southern society was presented as exhibiting a deep fear and hatred of blacks or black equality. It is easy to see why the average white reader, denied any real insight into the nature of other kinds of difficulties facing blacks in other areas of the country, would assume that once civil rights for blacks in the South were secured, most of the nation's racial problems would be solved.

During the 1970s the papers ran many more stories on a greater variety of black problems than they had before; a total of thirty-three such stories was found in the 116 issues coded. The papers also began, for almost the first time in all the coverage sampled, to present statistical information that showed the inequality that existed between blacks and whites in many areas of life. For instance, the *New York Times* reported that in 1980 blacks had a maternal death rate triple that of whites, an infant death rate twice that of whites, a life expectancy six years shorter than that of whites. The *Constitution* noted that blacks were four times as likely to die of heart disease than whites, five times more likely to die of tuberculosis, and twice as likely to die of diabetes.

The *Globe* ran a story on a 1978 Rand Corporation study that predicted it would be at least 30 years before black men's earnings equaled those of white men. The *Tribune* reported that in 1969 the median income of black families was 61 percent of white median income; by 1978 it had dropped to 59 percent of white family income. Various stories pointed out that unemployment among blacks of both sexes consistently remained higher than that of whites, while the unemployment rate for black teenagers was, by 1980, triple that for white youths. In 1978 a *Constitution* editorial about unemployment among black teenagers warned that "a society that tolerates a 38 percent unemployment rate in any large section of the population is indeed living in a fool's paradise." By late 1982 the unemployment rate of black youths had reached 50 percent.[8]

Several editorials observed that since the 1965 Freedom March and passage of the Voting Rights Act the number of blacks registered to vote in the Deep South had increased dramatically, with noticeable results. In 1962, the *Times* reported, no blacks served in the legislatures of these states; by 1974 there were 94 black state legislators, and the number of blacks who held elective office in the South had risen from less than 100 to 900 in the same period. But a *Times* editorial warned that as of 1974 positions held by blacks represented only 2 percent of the elective public offices in the South, voter registration among blacks was still low in seven southern states, and discrimination against would-be voting registrants still existed there.

Throughout the 1970s various stories and editorials in the issues sampled indicated that progress toward equality for blacks was slowing and that gains already made were being threatened. In 1980 the Civil Rights Commission stated that a package of legislative amendments then before Congress would nullify twenty-five years of civil rights achievements. In 1972 and again in 1978 various civil rights leaders were reported as saying that the cause of blacks was being abandoned nationally.

A 1980 *Constitution* story about the murder of black children in Atlanta, the recent slaying of blacks in other cities, and the light punishments for whites convicted of the killings said that blacks were both fearful and resentful of white indifference to the slayings and to the recent upsurge in white hate groups. Atlanta Mayor Maynard Jackson, commenting on the increased popularity of the Ku Klux Klan and similar groups, asked if whites would be indifferent if blacks "were running around with guns saying they were going to kill white folks and cops." Jackson said, "Mister, that would never have been tolerated." But he noted there seemed to be no outcry or outrage from the white community at the activities of anti-black hate groups.

Whatever weaknesses might be ascribed to the papers' 1970s coverage of black problems—that there still was not enough of it, that it was not locally oriented, and that it did not include enough coverage of the situation in the ghettos—it is nonetheless encouraging that the papers had come to realize that serious problems still existed and were attempting to inform their readers about them.

COVERAGE OF CAUSES OF PROTEST

The Kerner Commission and journalists themselves had suggested that the press did not cover the causes of social protest very

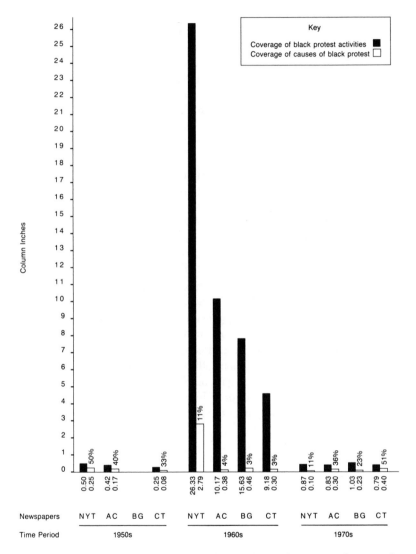

Figure 4. Mean number of column inches per issue of coverage of causes of black protest activities as percentage of total coverage of black protest activities in four newspapers during three time periods

thoroughly during the 1960s, and the findings presented in Figure 4 support this contention. The figure shows the amount of space each newspaper devoted, as a percentage of its coverage of black protest activities, to coverage of the causes of the protests. During the 1960s, the period when they ran the largest amount of coverage of black protest, the papers gave explanation of the causes of the protests the smallest amounts of space—between 3 and 11 percent of their total coverage of protests. In both the 1950s and the 1970s the coverage of causes ran higher, as a percentage of total protest coverage, in most of the papers.

The newspapers' scanty explanation of the causes of black protest during the 1960s, plus their relative inattention to black problems, combined to convey a picture suggesting that blacks were aggressive and demanding. During this period the newspapers presented blacks as demonstrating, staging sit-ins, making demands, and issuing warnings about long, hot summers, but since so little background was given on the reasons why they felt their actions were necessary, their side of the story did not emerge clearly.

A good example of the papers' inattention to the causes of protest was the 1965 Selma-to-Montgomery march led by Dr. King to encourage blacks to register to vote in Alabama and to dramatize the difficulties they encountered in doing so. The *New York Times* devoted most of its front page and all of an inside page to extensive coverage of this event, running mood pieces and stories on sympathy marches in other cities, President Johnson's federalizing of the Alabama national guard to protect the marchers, the southerner in command of the guardsmen, and the hotline connecting the law enforcement officers with Washington.

Nowhere in all these numerous inches of coverage did the *Times* explain that the number of blacks then registered to vote in Alabama was less than 10 percent of those eligible, nor did it describe the violence and other reprisals that befell blacks who had tried to register, both in the past and currently. Aside from mentioning briefly white attacks on voting rights demonstrators in Selma the week before, and the clubbing to death of a protester, the *Times* provided no background at all on the long-standing and flagrant injustices that prompted the march. The reader was given abundant information on every aspect of the march, it seemed, except an explanation of why the marchers felt their pilgrimage was necessary.

A similar focus on facts and events rather than explanation of causes was found in all the papers studied in nearly all the stories on black protest activities coded from this period. It seemed as though the papers regarded the civil rights movement as a kind of drama to be followed and described, rather than as a manifestation of a severe societal maladjustment that cried out for thorough exploration and discussion by the media.

Several other notable examples of the same kind of inattention to the causes of 1960s black protests, combined with an overemphasis on conflict, were found. For example, the headline and lead of a 1963 *New York Times* story claimed that black militancy was growing in Jackson, Mississippi. No confirmation of this claim was offered besides the information that three civil rights groups said they planned to send representatives to Jackson. Not until twenty-two inches down in the story, after the article had been jumped to another page, did the reporter present the reason for this activity—the recent murder of Medgar Evers. In 1965, a *Times* story headlined "Boston Negroes Invade 4 Schools" reported that black parents had attempted peacefully to enroll their children in predominantly white schools. No invasion occurred; no explanation for the parents' action was offered.

The most blatant example of a *Times*' reporter's disinterest in— and even hostility toward—the motivations of black protesters was found in a 1967 story on an open housing demonstration in Louisville, where the Kentucky Derby was to be held the following week. The reporter, who had presented only half an inch of explanation of the cause of the demonstration, ended his story with the statement that Dr. King and Dick Gregory would arrive in town early the next week "to help in efforts *to ruin the occasion* [the Derby] for the thousands of people expected in town."9

Such coverage provides some justification for the Kerner Commission's claim that the press reflected white society's indifference and biases toward blacks. By failing to explain the causes of black protest, and focusing on the threatening nature of blacks' activities and demands, the papers presented an incomplete and possibly prejudicial picture of the black struggle for equality during the 1960s.

Both surprising and encouraging was the finding that in the 1970s issues sampled all the papers except the *New York Times* devoted a greater percentage of their coverage of black protests to explanations of the causes of the protests. This new emphasis on causes may have arisen partly from a conscious effort on the part of journalists to improve their coverage in this area. But it also may have been a reflection of Paletz and Dunn's contention that the media serve to maintain sociocultural consensus and tend to cover unfavorably those who threaten the status quo.

Perhaps in the 1960s, when the confrontational tactics of the civil rights movement had led to numerous disturbances across the nation, journalists saw black protesters as threats to the stability of society and unconsciously made little effort to explain the causes of their protests. Then in the 1970s, when interracial violence had subsided, perhaps reporters no longer saw blacks as threats and thus were willing to explain their grievances more fully. This same attitude may account for the proportionately greater attention the papers gave to the causes of black protests in the 1950s, when blacks were so thoroughly suppressed in American society that they were not seen as dangerous.

LOCATION OF CONFLICTS COVERED

The discussions of racial coverage in the 1960s had suggested that the press tended to concentrate on racial conflicts in other areas of the country while ignoring local racial tensions whenever possible, but the findings presented in Figure 5 offer no clear information about this contention. The figure shows what percentage of the coverage of conflict-oriented racial activities concerned events in each newspaper's own circulation area.

The percentages shown here vary widely and are strongly affected by the sample dates chosen. When the date of an issue sampled fell shortly after a Harlem riot in 1964, for instance, or coincided with the first day of school desegregation in Boston in 1974, the coverage of these events pushed up the local newspaper's totals in the local conflict category.

Some observations on the content of the coverage, however, suggest that the papers did tend to emphasize the controversial aspects of racial confrontations in other cities while taking a more moderate tone in coverage of local situations. The most outstanding example was found in the 1974 sample issues that covered the first day of desegregated school in Boston.

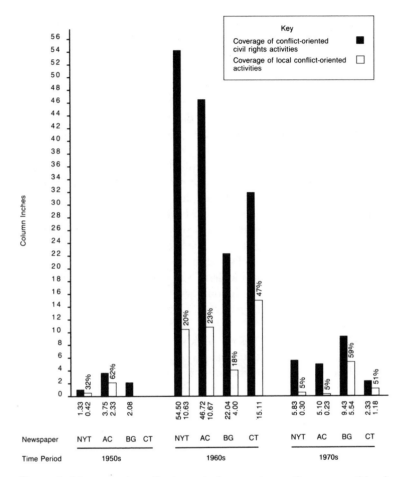

Figure 5. Mean number of column inches per issue of coverage of local conflict-oriented civil rights events as percentage of total coverage of conflict-oriented civil rights events in four newspapers during three time periods

The *Boston Globe*'s banner headline for that day read "Boston Schools Desegregated, Opening Day Generally Peaceful." All the extensive coverage in that issue of the *Globe* emphasized that the overwhelming majority of Boston schools were integrated without incident, the single exception occurring at South Boston High

School, where anti-busing demonstrators shouted insults at black students entering the predominantly white school and stoned the buses carrying the black students when school ended.

In contrast, the *New York Times* story on this same event was headlined "Violence Mars Busing in Boston," while that of the *Constitution* said "Busing Met by Violence in Boston." The *Chicago Tribune*'s main front-page photo that day was of an injured policeman who had fallen to the ground, and the photo's head said "Policeman Hurt in Boston Busing Fight." The *Tribune*'s story, like those of the other two papers, emphasized the conflict angle of the day's events.[10]

Another example concerned the previously mentioned incident in Boston in 1965, when black parents, in their efforts to hasten desegregation of the schools, arranged to have 300 black children transported to five less crowded white schools, where they managed to get 85 of the children registered. The headline of the *Times'* story on this event claimed that blacks had invaded the schools. By contrast, the *Globe* coverage of the incident was moderate in tone, was not conflict-oriented, and was the only story among all those coded in the 1960s in which all the reported white response to black protest activities was *positive*.

In both of these examples the *Globe*'s calm approach to coverage of the events could be construed as playing down local racial conflicts as much as possible. On the other hand, it could be considered a more accurate presentation of what actually occurred than the other papers' more conflict-focused approaches.

Related to the matter of emphasizing the racial troubles of other parts of the country was the newspapers' practice of sending their own reporters to cover distant racial conflicts. For example, in 1965 both the *New York Times* and *Boston Globe* sent their own reporters to cover the Selma-to-Montgomery march. The *Chicago Tribune* issue for this date was not available for coding. In contrast, the *Atlanta Constitution* carried only a UPI story on this event, which occurred less than 200 miles away. The *Globe* also sent a reporter South to cover the later trial of the men charged with beating a civil rights demonstrator to death in Selma the week before the march.

During the 1970s the *Constitution* had an opportunity to reciprocate; it sent a reporter to Boston to cover the first day of school desegregation. The reporter noted in his lead that "the sometimes violent encounter" between police and protesters in Boston "was in sharp contrast to most school desegregation in Georgia, marked by strong opposition but little serious physical conflict."[11]

In another issue the *Constitution* announced that it would run a three-part series on the integration problems that led to a white boycott of many schools in Brooklyn. The stories also would report, the announcement said, on the difference in the way the New York and Atlanta school systems were coping with desegregation. These examples suggest that the newspapers did, indeed, tend to emphasize the racial conflicts in other cities and areas of the country and that they did not necessarily ignore, but perhaps soft-pedaled, racial troubles in their own cities.

EDITORIAL COVERAGE

Table 3 presents the themes of all the editorials about blacks found in the issues sampled. This information is included here to help describe each newspaper's editorial attitude toward blacks and to show how these attitudes changed over time.

The major finding presented in this table is that during the 1960s all of the newspapers, except the *Chicago Tribune*, expressed sympathy for the aims of the civil rights movement, and they continued to evidence editorial support for the black struggle for equality during the 1970s. Conversely, the *Tribune* demonstrated strong editorial opposition to moves to end segregation during the 1960s, and in its 1970s editorials sampled showed less hostility toward equality for blacks but still exhibited more concern with preserving the status quo than with correcting injustices.

Several aspects of Table 3 are worthy of note. One is that only two editorials concerning blacks were run in the issues sampled from the 1950s, and although these expressed no hostility toward blacks, they were not strongly sympathetic either. For example, the *Boston Globe* editorial in the 1950s supported efforts to establish a national Fair Employment Practices Commission because the move would improve the U.S. image abroad and enable more people to work in war industries; the paper's support of the idea was based entirely on practical reasons, and no mention was made of ethical considerations or racial justice.

It is interesting to note that the theme of the *Atlanta Constitution* editorial run in the 1950s, which criticized a political candidate for

Table 3
Themes of Editorials About Blacks Found in Issues Coded of Four
Newspapers During Three Time Periods

Time Period	News-paper	Theme	Number run on theme
1950s	AC	Local politician criticized for attempting to discredit opponent by showing opponent shaking hands with blacks.	1
	BG	Congressional efforts to establish FEPC approved.	1
1960s	NYT	Achievements of Carl Stokes, Carl Rowan honored.	2
		New York City mayor praised for firmness in time of racial tension.	1
		Continuation of local police civilian review board supported so that voices of all citizens will be heard.	1
		Mississippi police should protect peaceful civil rights demonstrators.	1
	AC	Blacks should have equitable participation in the economic system.	1
		It is wrong to bar people from civilized treatment in places of public accommodation.	1
		Barring blacks from churches is an affront to Christian principles.	1
		Peaceful civil rights demonstrators should be protected by the police.	1
		Would-be voter registrants should be protected.	1
		Blacks should be allowed to vote.	3
		Southern callousness toward poor, toward black victims of white violence, criticized.	2
		Blacks urged to be reasonable in demands during negotiations to improve city's black schools.	1
	BG	Political leaders should take action to alleviate the problems that cause riots, persistent discrimination.	4
		Poor Peoples' Marchers should be given protection, chance to be heard.	1
		Black parents who tried to register their children in local white schools supported.	1
	CT	Most citizens, including blacks, want strong police force.	2
		Justice Dept. criticized for ordering Illinois community to desegregate schools.	2
		Milwaukee judge criticized for refusal to allow referendum on open housing.	1
		Student protesters are being used by outside agitators.	1
		FEPC examiner criticized for ordering firm to hire black applicant who failed examination.	1
		Prince Edward County, Va., criticized for closing public schools to integrate them.	1

TABLE 3 - - continued

Time Period	News-paper	Theme	Number run on theme
1970s	NYT	Effort of minorities to have more voice in local city council decision making supported.	1
		Layoffs in city's financial crisis have hurt minorities most, but abandoning seniority in determining who to fire would result in reverse discrimination.	1
		Interracial cooperation to save local park commended .	1
		All of society will benefit from spread of black influence in politics, business, labor, other power centers.	1
		Racial progress in U.S. is slow; much remains to be done.	2
		Awards to three men who fought racism commended.	1
	AC	State politician criticized for attempt to discredit opponent by showing opponent's supporters being friendly with black leaders.	1
		National program to train and educate jobless black teen-agers urged.	1
		Black voting, participation in politics encouraged.	1
		Disparity between haves and have-nots in America remains wide.	2
		Blacks should be encouraged to enter medical school.	1
		Actions of local black mayor approved.	2
	BG	City school committee must get on with task of racially balancing city schools.	1
		City can be proud of success of first day of school deseg-regation.	1
		Local police commissioner supported in statement that violence over school desegregation must cease.	1
		President Nixon criticized for retreating from leadership on civil rights.	1
		Rights of southern civil rights demonstrators supported.	1
	CT	Bill suspending busing to achieve school integration supported.	1
		State superintendent of education's failure to insist on busing students from city to suburbs approved.	1
		Union and federal guidlines for assigning teachers to city schools criticized.	1
		Use of quotas in hiring is "absurdly arbitrary."	1
		Black and white members of city school board should stop attacking each other.	1
		Black voters should free selves from "subservience" to Democratic machine.	1
		Would-be assassin of Vernon Jordan will surely prove to be madman.	1
		Segregation in housing, public schools in Chicago is firmly entrenched.	1
		Violence of Boston mobs protesting busing criticized.	1

attempting to damage his opponent by running ads showing his opponent being friendly with blacks, was repeated in another *Constitution* editorial two decades later. During the 1960s a theme that occurred in the editorials of all the newspapers except the *Tribune* was that peaceful civil rights demonstrators should be given police protection. The *Tribune* raised the law-and-order issue also, but from the viewpoint that strong police forces were needed to save law-abiding citizens from criminals and rioters.

Somehow the *Tribune*'s editorial writers always found a logical-sounding reason, in the 1960s issues sampled, for opposing school desegregation, an end to housing and employment discrimination, and student demonstrations. Thomas J. Kelly, in his study of Chicago newspapers' editorial opinions of the race problem during this period, described a stance that tallies exactly with the *Tribune*'s editorial position in the issues sampled. "Ignoring the country's racial inequalities until proposals for change were put forth," Kelly wrote, "the papers then proceeded to oppose the proposals and discredit those advocating change, regardless of the merit or militancy involved."

He also noted, "The *Tribune* ignored or bitterly criticized every proposal for civil rights legislation at the federal, state or local level, and vehemently opposed government welfare expenditures for the black and the poor." Meanwhile, he observed, the paper advocated government intervention to help the business community and the upper classes.[12] During the 1970s the *Tribune* editorials coded showed less hostility toward the black struggle for equality but continued to emphasize plausible-sounding reasons why moves to end school segregation and inequality in employment should be undertaken slowly and cautiously.

The editorials of the *New York Times* during the 1960s and 1970s repeated in several ways the idea that greater participation by black citizens in the life of the city and of the nation would benefit all citizens. Under the leadership of editor Ralph McGill, the *Atlanta Constitution*'s editorials in the 1960s presented a clear statement of support for civil rights for blacks. These kinds of themes continued into the 1970s. A topic frequently mentioned in this paper's editorials during both periods was encouragement of blacks being allowed to vote and of black participation in politics. The editorials of the *Boston Globe* during both the 1960s and the 1970s tended to call upon national political figures for leadership and action in civil rights.

OTHER SIMILARITIES IN COVERAGE

The newspapers displayed, especially during the 1960s, a few additional commonalities in their coverage of blacks that are worthy of note. During that period the papers showed a reluctance to present blacks—except those in the South—as victims of injustice and oppression, as deserving of compassion and help, either in stories devoted to explaining black problems or in news stories about programs to alleviate some of the difficulties facing blacks. For example, at this time legislation to establish employment training programs, summer youth projects, and other social welfare programs were often discussed and sometimes passed. Yet the stories on such legislation never indicated that blacks would be among those served by the programs, nor did they include minority income and employment statistics or other indications why the programs were needed.

Hartmann and Husband observed a similar situation in a failure by the British media to show colored immigrants as victims of racist attacks and oppression. The authors suggest that by placing an embargo on news that demonstrated British racism and oppression of immigrants, the British media thus acted to maintain sociocultural consensus by making sure that "the image of British 'tolerance' remained intact and the need to ask questions about the nature of British society was avoided."[13] A similar situation may have existed among American media during the 1960s.

To the credit of all the papers, except the *Chicago Tribune*, was their editorial support of the aims of the civil rights movement in the 1960s and their extensive coverage of white religious and political leaders' calls for integration, an end to racial hatred, and moderation. This coverage is shown in the white leaders' call for integration subcategory in Tables 4 through 7. The reports of both the McCone Commission, reporting on the causes of the Los Angeles riots, and the Kerner Commission also were given extensive space. The three newspapers' managements seemed to want to emphasize calls for equality and compassion and recommendations to improve the situation of blacks, and they expressed these ideas in their own editorials.

By these means the papers kept their readers reminded of the American ideals of equality and justice.

At the UCLA conference Gunnar Myrdal noted that in his 1944 book on blacks in American society he said that he viewed the race problem as fundamentally a moral dilemma within the heart of the white man. He pointed out that blacks then constituted only about a tenth of the nation's population and had "much less than a tenth of those things which give influence and power."

If the ideals and consciences of a large number of whites had not been on their side, Myrdal said, the situation of American blacks would have been less than hopeless.[14] This study's findings suggest that, despite numerous coverage weaknesses, the hearts and minds of the three newspapers' managements must have inclined strongly toward the justice—if not the methods—of the black man's cause during the 1960s.

A similar situation was observed in the 1970s coverage sampled. During this period the same three papers all covered, in both stories and editorials, instances of interracial cooperation and successful desegregation and provided continued editorial support for the ideals of racial equality. The managements of all three papers seemed to want to present examples of mutual assistance between the races, efforts to make integration work, and evidence that desegregation could be accomplished successfully.

ASSESSMENT OF NEWSPAPER PERFORMANCE

Perhaps the most significant finding of this study is that during the 1970s all the newspapers examined provided more, and more realistic, coverage of black Americans than they had during the 1950s or even, by some measures, during the 1960s. Coverage of blacks had risen sharply in the 1960s because of the events of the civil rights movement and the riots, but the coverage did not decline dramatically in the 1970s when these activities ceased. Instead, the coverage remained close to what it had been in the 1960s, in some papers surpassing what it was in that period in terms of column inches or percentage of available news space.

In addition, a greatly increased percentage of each paper's total coverage of blacks in the 1970s was devoted to items covering the normal life of the black community and showing blacks in the context of the total American society. Clearly the newspapers examined had moved, in the 1970s, in the direction of some of the coverage improvements suggested in the 1960s.

Also of some interest was the empirical support this study's findings provided for some of the criticisms of press coverage expressed by the Kerner Commission and journalists during the 1960s. The study showed, for example, that the papers examined largely neglected explanations of causes in their coverage of black protest events and of the civil rights movement in general, in the 1960s issues sampled.

The findings also indicated that the papers did not present much news about black Americans as part of the ordinary life of the community in the 1960s and ran even less of this type of news in the 1950s; the papers did ignore the plight of black citizens in the 1950s and ran comparatively little on black problems in the 1960s, in the issues coded; and their coverage of blacks in the 1950s and 1960s did reflect, in some ways, white society's indifference and distrust of black Americans. All these types of coverage deficiencies had been discussed, but not systematically studied, by journalists and the Kerner Commission in the 1960s.

In chapter 4 some discussion was presented of the kinds of newspaper coverage of American blacks and of race relations that might measure up to the social responsibility standards proposed by the Hutchins Commission and that might alleviate the coverage weaknesses noted by the Kerner Commission and the journalists who discussed press coverage of these areas. It was suggested that, first of all, newspapers should cover the same kinds of news about blacks as they do about whites. They should present a picture of the ordinary activities of the black community as well as of the unusual, it was thought, and they should avoid overemphasis on stereotypical kinds of coverage.

The findings of this project suggest that all the newspapers studied made considerable progress in this area during the 1970s and began to provide a much more complete and representative portrayal of black life than they had in the two earlier periods studied. Three of the papers did, however, increase their coverage of stereotypical activities in the 1970s.

It was thought that improved coverage of black Americans would include explanation of the many obstacles to the efforts of blacks, especially those who live in ghettos, to enjoy social and economic opportunity in this country. Here again, all the newspapers except the *Boston Globe* showed great improvement in problem coverage during the 1970s, running much more coverage of a much wider array of black problems than they had in the two previous periods.

The study's findings indicated, however, that the papers' coverage of black problems could be further improved in several ways. One of these would be providing more attention to the problems facing local blacks, and another would be presenting a clearer picture of the frustrations experienced by the more than half of the nation's black citizens who live in inner-city ghettos.

The discussion of ideal coverage suggested that newspapers should do a better job than they had done during the 1960s in explaining the causes of black protest. In this area, the papers studied showed an improvement in the 1970s over their performance in the 1960s. But the *New York Times* stories continued to focus on facts, quotes, and numbers in their coverage of social protest in the 1970s and largely failed to explain the underlying causes.

Finally, the discussion of improved coverage suggested that the newspapers should eliminate indications of indifference and antipathy toward black Americans. This seems to have been largely accomplished in the 1970s coverage by the newspapers studied. Except for the difficulties mentioned in the preceding paragraphs, news about blacks seemed to be handled the same as news about whites in this period.

LIMITATIONS OF THE STUDY

The major limitation of this study is that its findings are not generalizable to other newspapers. Instead, the findings represent the coverage patterns of only the four newspapers examined, although these may well suggest some general trends among American newspapers. In addition, the papers used in the study are among the nation's largest and richest, and in these ways they are atypical. It is possible that a study of other leading American newspapers for the same time periods might produce similar findings about press attention to blacks in the 1970s, while a study of smaller papers might produce opposite results.

The time periods chosen for the study proved to be a great advantage; studying coverage of American blacks in three such different periods in the nation's history provided numerous contrasts that helped to produce some definite conclusions. A larger sample size for the 1950s period studied, however, might have provided the researcher with more coverage examples to flesh out the explanation of the numerical data.

Another limitation of the study was that it was not possible to catch every item about American blacks in every sample issue. Because newspapers seldom identify blacks as blacks any longer, often the researcher must already know whether a person—such as an entertainer or political figure—being mentioned in a story is black or not. Also, many of the people mentioned in stories about local events probably were black, but the researcher had no way of knowing when this was the case and thus doubtless failed to code some relevant stories.

Generally speaking, however, the study seemed to catch in its net most items about American blacks in the issues sampled, and the data obtained provide some interesting and valuable insights into the manner in which the four newspapers covered blacks during the periods under study.

NOTES

1. See Simpson, p. 6; Johnson, Sears, and McConahay, p. 707.

2. Johnson, Sears, and McConahay, p. 707.

3. Secrest, p. 100.

4. Johnson, Sears, and McConahay, pp. 707, 712.

5. Ibid., pp. 712, 711.

6. Dalsimer and Klein, in Fisher and Lowenstein, *Race and the News Media*, pp. 114, 141.

7. Warren Wheat, "It Was a Little Thing, But It Gave Hope," in Gannett News Service, *Equality: America's Unfinished Business*, p. 7.

8. Alexander, p. 54.

9. Douglas Robinson, "Louisville Demonstrators Turn Attention to Affluent East Side," *New York Times*, 25 April 1967, p. 29; emphasis added.

10. Further information on the way out-of-town media emphasized the violence of Boston's first day of school integration will be described in chapter 8.

11. Beau Cutts, "Busing Met by Violence in Boston," *Atlanta Constitution*, 13 Sept. 1974, p. 1.

12. Kelly, pp. 429–32.

13. Hartmann and Husband, pp. 174–77.

14. Gunnar Myrdal, "The Racial Crisis in Perspective," in Lyle, *The Black American and the Press*, p. 7.

CHAPTER 7

Individual Newspapers' Coverage

Although the study's major findings were presented in the preceding chapter, much additional useful information can be obtained from examining in greater detail how the individual newspapers covered American blacks during the time periods examined.

The data provided in this chapter offer some valuable insights into the way the media's difficulties—and good intentions—in reporting racial matters are translated into specific coverage. In addition, the changes in the newspapers' coverage of American blacks over the three time periods and the examples of actual coverage are interesting in themselves, and some of the coverage also is entertaining.

COVERAGE BY THE NEW YORK TIMES

Perhaps the most outstanding characteristic of the *New York Times'* coverage of American blacks was that this newspaper evidenced leadership during all three periods in providing coverage of the problems experienced by black citizens, as Figure 2 illustrates. In addition, during the 1970s this paper ran nearly three times as many column inches per issue of coverage of problems than it had in the previous periods, as Table 4 shows, and explored a variety of difficulties facing black Americans, from those of blacks living in ghettos to those of professional persons (see Appendix C).

The *Times* consistently gave little attention to black crime and showed a definite focus on civil rights–related matters, as is illustrated in Table 4. During both the 1950s and 1960s, in the issues sampled, the *Times* concentrated on civil rights activities, and in the 1970s the paper's coverage in this area decreased, but its coverage of blacks in every other subcategory rose.

Table 4

Mean Number of Column Inches Per Issue of Coverage of Black Americans by Subcategories of Coverage in the *New York Times* During Three Time Periods

Coverage	Time Period		
	1950s	1960s	1970s
Stereotypical			
Antisocial activities	0.33 (2%)	2.33 (2%)	4.74 (5%)
Entertainment figures	1.50 (8%)	4.58 (3%)	8.56 (9%)
Subtotal	1.83 (10%)	6.92 (5%)	13.31 (14%)
Everyday Life			
Community activities	0.50 (3%)	9.58 (7%)	19.82 (21%)
Individual achievements	2.75 (15%)	5.42 (4%)	9.16 (10%)
Political activities		10.08 (7%)	12.03 (12%)
Local officeholders at work			1.27 (1%)
Disasters		0.21	3.82 (4%)
Interracial violence		2.63 (2%)	1.04 (1%)
Subtotal	3.25 (18%)	27.92 (19%)	47.14 (49%)
Civil Rights - Related			
Protest	0.50 (3%)	26.33 (18%)	0.86 (1%)
Riot/Community tense		7.67 (5%)	1.13 (1%)
White resistance to integration	0.83 (5%)	20.50 (14%)	3.82 (4%)
Civil rights gains	4.50 (25%)	9.08 (6%)	2.76 (3%)
Civil rights - related activities	4.25 (23%)	30.63 (21%)	13.22 (14%)
White leaders call for integration		15.00 (10%)	
Subtotal	10.08 (56%)	109.21 (74%)	21.98 (23%)
Minority Life			
Problems	1.83 (10%)	3.58 (2%)	10.37 (11%)
Housing programs	1.33 (7%)		4.18 (4%)
Subtotal	3.16 (17%)	3.58 (2%)	14.55 (15%)
Total	18.33 (100%)	147.63 (100%)	96.98 (100%)

During both the 1960s and 1970s the *Times* devoted more column inches to coverage of blacks than did any of the other newspapers (see Table 1). More than any of the other papers, the *Times* ran news of blacks in its financial, society, and obituary pages during the 1970s. Its per-issue average coverage of everyday-life activities of blacks in the 1970s was almost double what it had been in the 1960s.

In the 1960s the few *Times* editorials concerning blacks found in the issues coded expressed a positive attitude toward the aims of the civil rights movement, but this was belied to some extent by the occasional sensationalism and insensitivity toward the causes of black protest displayed in news coverage during this period. The *Times* continued, in the 1970s issues sampled, its editorial support of equal rights and opportunities for blacks and encouraged black participation in all fields of power and decision making.

COVERAGE BY THE *ATLANTA CONSTITUTION*

The most noteworthy aspect of the *Atlanta Constitution*'s coverage of blacks during all three periods was that the paper consistently devoted a larger proportion of its news hole to coverage of blacks than did any of the other newspapers, as shown in Figure 1. The *Constitution* may have covered blacks more extensively partly because Atlanta had a much larger percentage of blacks in its population than did the other cities during the three periods studied.

As Table 5 shows, in all three time periods examined, the *Constitution* devoted a fair proportion of its coverage of blacks to items about everyday-life activities. During the 1950s the paper provided the largest amount of everyday-life coverage of all the papers and also paid a considerable amount of attention to crimes committed by blacks. In one of the sample issues from this period, the paper ran a column entitled "Our Negro Community," which presented news about local black organizations, and on several other occasions this paper ran stories on the accomplishments of local blacks, suggesting that the paper's management accepted an obligation to provide some coverage of the everyday life of the local black community.

In the 1960s issues coded, the *Constitution* ran many editorials expressing strong sympathy for some of the problems of blacks and support for the aims of the civil rights movement, even though the

Table 5

Mean Number of Column Inches Per Issue of Coverage of Black Americans by Subcategories of Coverage in the *Atlanta Constitution* During Three Time Periods

Coverage	Time Period		
	1950s	1960s	1970s
Stereotypical			
Antisocial actions	4.42 (20%)	3.60 (5%)	11.85 (13%)
Entertainment figures	0.42 (2%)	0.68 (1%)	3.71 (5%)
Subtotal	4.83 (22%)	4.28 (6%)	15.56 (18%)
Everyday Life			
Community activities	3.08 (14%)	2.43 (3%)	17.50 (20%)
Individual achievements	1.67 (7%)	0.65 (1%)	6.87 (8%)
Political activities	0.50 (2%)	5.74 (8%)	9.28 (10%)
Local officeholders at work			8.50 (10%)
Disasters	2.67 (12%)	1.46 (2%)	4.25 (5%)
Interracial violence			2.31 (3%)
Subtotal	7.92 (35%)	10.27 (14%)	48.71 (55%)
Civil Rights - Related			
Protest	0.42 (2%)	10.17 (13%)	0.82 (1%)
Riot/Community tense		1.62 (2%)	
White resistance to integration	3.33 (15%)	12.38 (16%)	4.28 (5%)
Civil rights gains	2.00 (9%)	3.41 (5%)	0.37
Civil rights - related activities	3.08 (14%)	16.24 (21%)	8.48 (10%)
White leaders call for integration		8.36 (11%)	1.11 (1%)
Subtotal	8.83 (40%)	52.17 (69%)	15.07 (17%)
Minority Life			
Problems		3.63 (5%)	8.09 (9%)
Housing programs	1.00 (4%)	5.41 (7%)	1.07 (1%)
Subtotal	1.00 (4%)	9.04 (12%)	9.16 (10%)
Total	22.58 (100%)	75.77 (100%)	88.48 (100%)

paper was located in an area of the country where such views were not popular. Editor Ralph McGill was subjected to frequent harassment for his editorial stands as early as the late 1950s and was often vilified by the Georgia equivalent of the White Citizens Council publication. He wrote that he particularly treasured a 1957 issue of the publication that carried a banner headline reading "Ralph McGill Menace to Georgia: South's Worst Foe Since Thad Stevens."[1]

Despite the *Constitution*'s editorial sympathy with the aims of the civil rights revolution in the 1960s, however, in the news pages of the paper a different attitude toward blacks—particularly local blacks—seemed to prevail. Although the population of Atlanta during this period was more than 38 percent black, almost no news about local black organizations, churches, or schools was found in the issues coded. The only type of news about local blacks that appeared regularly in the issues sampled from this period was stories about crimes committed by blacks and, to a smaller extent, news about blacks involved in auto accidents. News about local blacks did not appear elsewhere in the paper except in the "Colored" section of the obituary page.

Other types of insensitivity toward blacks were occasionally evidenced in the *Constitution*'s coverage in the 1960s. In one instance the paper, reporting a particularly brutal kidnapping and rape of a black girl by six youths, omitted mention of the rapists' race. Since the paper consistently, at this time, identified all black wrongdoers as "Negro," it was obvious that the youths were white. This was just one of the many examples found in which all the newspapers studied, both during the 1950s and the 1960s, seemed to downplay as much as possible the victimization of ordinary blacks—as opposed to black civil rights demonstrators—by whites.

Signs of progress were evident, however. By 1968 the *Constitution* had dropped the designation "Negro" in crime and accident stories and obituaries. In that year the paper began running a fourteen-part series on "The Two Atlantas." The stories presented a history of blacks in Atlanta, their family structure; their outlook on jobs, education, and politics; their relations with police; their leaders; and other topics. The series clearly represented a major commitment of the paper's resources to coverage of local blacks and also, perhaps, indicated a major readjustment in the *Constitution* management's attitude toward them.

Even earlier in the 1960s the *Constitution* had run a story on a successful black voter registration drive in a nearby county. The drive was initiated by county officials and was not a response to pressure by a civil rights group. An editorial lauded this program as an example of white southerners doing the right thing on their own initiative. In this and other articles the paper seemed not only to present a positive attitude toward desegregation but also to show how it could be accomplished smoothly.

In the 1970s issues coded, the *Constitution*'s coverage of everyday-life activities accounted for four times as many column inches per issue as it had in the previous period studied. During the late 1970s the mayor of Atlanta was black, as were the chief of police and many members of the city council. Ten percent of the *Constitution*'s coverage of everyday-life activities of blacks during this period concerned these local officeholders doing their jobs.

Also indicative of the *Constitution* management's apparent increasing acceptance of blacks as a part of the city's normal life were several features on local blacks and a piece asking, "Where are the local black audiences for the performing arts?" This was the only piece found among all 1,241 items coded that explored the cultural background and interests of blacks, particularly the black middle class.

The *Constitution*'s per-issue average of coverage of black problems in the 1970s doubled over what it had been in the previous period, as Table 5 shows. Also, during this time the paper continued its editorial support of black equality and warned, in both editorials and numerous stories on black problems, that such equality had by no means been achieved.

COVERAGE BY THE BOSTON GLOBE

The *Boston Globe*'s coverage was outstanding for its calm and positive approach to local school integration efforts in both the 1960s and 1970s issues coded. More than any of the other papers studied, the *Globe* seemed to identify itself with the aims of blacks on this issue and to involve itself in efforts to make desegregation work.

Table 6

Mean Number of Column Inches Per Issue of Coverage of Black
Americans by Subcategories of Coverage in the *Boston Globe* During
Three Time Periods

Coverage	Time Period		
	1950s	1960s	1970s
Stereotypical			
Antisocial actions		1.40 (2%)	3.01 (3%)
Entertainment figures		1.40 (2%)	4.30 (5%)
Subtotal		2.80 (4%)	7.31 (8%)
Everyday Life			
Community activities		3.30 (5%)	7.44 (9%)
Individual achievements	0.78 (17%)	1.64 (2%)	6.09 (7%)
Political activities		2.56 (4%)	2.93 (3%)
Local officeholders at work			4.02 (5%)
Disasters			0.47
Interracial violence			4.98 (6%)
Subtotal	0.78 (17%)	7.50 (11%)	25.92 (30%)
Civil Rights - Related			
Protest		15.60 (24%)	1.03 (1%)
Riot/Community tense		1.33 (2%)	0.62
White resistance to integration		5.08 (8%)	7.78 (9%)
Civil rights gains	0.33 (8%)	1.43 (2%)	12.03 (14%)
Civil rights - related activities	3.44 (76%)	15.81 (24%)	27.38 (32%)
White leaders call for integration		12.44 (19%)	1.58 (2%)
Subtotal	3.77 (84%)	51.69 (79%)	50.42 (58%)
Minority Life			
Problems		3.65 (5%)	2.67 (3%)
Housing programs		0.52 (1%)	0.52
Subtotal		4.17 (6%)	3.19 (3%)
Total	4.55 (100%)	66.14 (100%)	86.85 (100%)

In the 1950s issues coded, the *Globe*'s coverage of black Americans was noteworthy primarily because only four items about blacks were found in the nine issues sampled. This paucity of coverage is indicated in Table 6. In this period the *Globe*, of all the papers, devoted by far the smallest proportion of its news hole to blacks, as Figure 1 shows.

The paper's coverage of blacks during the 1960s seemed sympathetic, although the *Globe* still provided less coverage of blacks than any of the other newspapers. The paper displayed a pro–civil rights editorial stance, evidenced no insensitivity toward blacks in its story and head placement, and displayed considerable understanding in both its news and editorial coverage of the previously mentioned black efforts to integrate Boston schools in 1965. The *Globe* coverage of that incident was moderate in tone and focused on the positive aspects of the situation. The paper supplemented its news coverage of the event with an editorial expressing understanding of the black parents' frustration and castigating the school board for stonewalling on integration.

During the 1970s, the *Globe*, like the first two papers discussed, continued its editorial support of equality for blacks and dramatically increased its per-issue average of coverage of everyday-life activities. It also was one of the papers whose coverage of blacks increased as a percentage of available news space in the 1970s over the 1960s, although to some extent this increase was caused by one of the sample dates falling on the first day of school desegregation. The *Globe*'s extensive coverage of this event accounted for 56 percent of its total coverage of blacks in the 1970s issues sampled. The *Globe* was the only one of the four newspapers whose coverage of black problems dropped rather than increased during this period.

In many ways the *Globe*'s coverage of the opening day of school desegregation in Boston in 1974 seemed to be a model of the kind of approach to coverage of racial conflict that had been suggested by journalists during the 1960s. The paper's coverage of the day's events was characterized by moderation, thoroughness, and emphasis on the positive.

The front-page banner headline that day reported that Boston schools had been desegregated and the opening day was generally peaceful. The main photo showed, not a rock thrower, but black and white children making friends on a playground. The lead story said that "despite boycotts and one incident of violence, the opening day was generally free of conflict." It added that threats of a citywide boycott and predictions of violence had largely failed to materialize. The second lead story reported Boston Mayor Kevin White ordering increased police protection and other measures to insure black students' safety and saying that the people of Boston would not tolerate a repetition of the day's stoning of buses in South Boston. He added that the overwhelming majority of schools were integrated without incident. The story went on to describe the previous summer's efforts by numerous community groups to insure that school desegregation would work.

Below these stories were two articles headlined "Real Heroes Were the Children." The articles described the experiences of a black youth who had attended South Boston High School that day and those of a white youth who went to a predominantly black high school in Roxbury. The only negative news on the front page was a report on a local NAACP official telling angry black parents to keep their children home from South Boston schools until the police proved they could protect them.

The inside pages continued the same focus on the positive that the front page had provided. One very long story emphasizing that problems were minor at most schools provided anecdotes on opening day experiences at each school. Another described the dignity of the black teenagers entering South Boston High School despite the insults hurled at them.

A third story was written by a reporter who mixed with the demonstrators outside the school, and the article portrayed the different kinds of people who made up the crowd and explained their various reasons for protesting. Still another story described the mayor's experiences that day, and another presented those of the city school superintendent. An editorial entitled "A Fine Beginning" mentioned some of the positive incidents that occurred and said the city could be proud of the success of the opening day. In the entire paper only one photo showed a negative incident—a youth throwing an egg at a bus.

The *Globe*'s extensive coverage of the opening day events was noteworthy in several respects. Instead of focusing its coverage on the small amount of conflict that occurred on opening day, the *Globe* emphasized the positive fact that the majority of the schools were integrated without incident. This was the only time in all the issues coded that a newspaper focused on *good* news when bad news was available, except for the 1965 school integration attempt reported by this same paper.

In addition, the *Globe* went far beyond a spot-news approach in its coverage of the day's events. It had made advance arrangements to interview the two youths who went to new high schools and the principals of all the newly integrated schools and to have reporters spend the day with the mayor and school superintendent. In addition, while the *Globe* did not neglect to explain the various motivations and rationales of the anti-busing demonstrators, it presented a sympathetic view of black youths braving white hostility to attend newly integrated schools. Another noticeable focus of the *Globe*'s coverage was its emphasis on efforts to make desegregation work and on interracial cooperation. This was evident in the opening day coverage, which emphasized successful desegregation, and in later stories about interracial cooperation.

Finally, the *Globe* coverage gave the impression, noticed for the first time in all the items coded, that many powerful forces in the city were committed wholeheartedly to making school desegregation a success. The coverage in the opening day issue and later ones conveyed clearly that the mayor, the police chief, the school superintendent, many community groups, and the *Globe* management itself believed in the cause of school desegregation and were determined to do all they could to make it work. This treatment was in stark contrast to all the other conflict-oriented stories coded in the study, which presented a picture of blacks struggling to achieve their aims against the indifference or hostility of the entrenched powers in the community and nation.

An ironic footnote to the *Globe*'s school desegregation coverage was provided by Edwin Diamond in an early 1975 *Columbia Journalism Review* article. Diamond said the two Boston newspapers' preparations for covering the opening day "should have earned the respect and approval of thoughtful professionals, if not blind partisans." Instead, he noted, "Press credibility suffered, and the Boston media, trying to perform the way the press is always being told to perform in crises, came under attack themselves in the Boston busing story."

The anti-busing forces claimed that the media were in collusion with city hall and school officials to inflate attendance figures and downplay racial incidents, Diamond said, and *Time* magazine warned of the "danger in self-censorship" and "news management." One critic charged that the *Globe* was "operating on a policy bordering on suppression" and suggested that the paper's decision to cover the first day of busing "with careful, detailed guidelines put it into a difficult position." The critic added, "Had everything been played straight everyone . . . might have benefitted."

The *Globe* had more than fifty reporters covering the opening day story, Diamond said, and he quoted a *Globe* executive who said, "When you have forty-eight reporters phone in and forty-seven of them say all is quiet while one reports trouble, what do you think the lead is?"[2] Apparently the critic quoted above would have answered that the lead is the trouble—that focusing on the violence would have been "playing it straight."

COVERAGE BY THE CHICAGO TRIBUNE

The *Chicago Tribune*'s coverage was notable for the hostility toward blacks and the aims of the civil rights movement evidenced in both the paper's news coverage and editorials in the first two time periods studied. Although the paper's editorial attitude moderated somewhat in the 1970s issues coded, the editorials continued to express extreme distrust toward any alteration of the status quo.

The paper's news coverage of blacks in the 1970s issues, however, exhibited definite and positive changes. During this period the paper reduced its emphasis on black crime and gave much more attention than it had previously to covering black problems and running news and pictures showing blacks as part of the everyday life of the community.

As was mentioned earlier, in the 1950s issues coded, the *Tribune* devoted 41 percent of its coverage of blacks to news about black crime (see Table 7). In addition, nearly all of the paper's coverage in the everyday-life category in this period was in the disasters subcategory; the paper ran photos of Chicago-area servicemen killed or missing in action in Korea, and 28 percent of these were blacks. Blacks comprised 14 percent of the city's population at the time.

Perhaps the best indication of the *Tribune* management's attitude toward blacks in the early 1950s was a story about the poor housing

Table 7

Mean Number of Column Inches Per Issue of Coverage of Black Americans by Subcategories of Coverage in the *Chicago Tribune* During Three Time Periods

Coverage	Time Period		
	1950s	1960s	1970s
Stereotypical			
Antisocial actions	13.08 (41%)	16.89 (17%)	4.76 (6%)
Entertainment figures	1.92 (6%)		7.32 (9%)
Subtotal	15.00 (47%)	16.89 (17%)	12.08 (15%)
Everyday Life			
Community activities	1.50 (5%)	1.18 (1%)	19.11 (24%)
Individual achievements		7.93 (8%)	10.45 (13%)
Political activities		4.22 (4%)	8.40 (11%)
Local officeholders at work			
Disasters	6.50 (20%)		4.09 (5%)
Interracial violence	0.42 (1%)	1.71 (2%)	1.00 (1%)
Subtotal	8.42 (26%)	15.04 (15%)	43.03 (54%)
Civil Rights - Related			
Protest	0.25 (1%)	9.18 (9%)	0.79 (1%)
Riot/Community tense		6.22 (6%)	
White resistance to integration	1.83 (6%)	16.52 (16%)	1.54 (2%)
Civil rights gains		1.93 (2%)	
Civil rights - related activities	2.25 (7%)	31.63 (31%)	12.40 (16%)
White leaders call for integration		5.18 (5%)	
Subtotal	4.33 (14%)	70.66 (69%)	14.72 (18%)
Minority Life			
Problems			10.00 (13%)
Housing programs	4.25 (13%)		
Subtotal	4.25 (13%)		10.00 (13%)
Total	32.00 (100%)	102.59 (100%)	79.83 (100%)

conditions in the city for migrants. Internal evidence in the article, some of which is quoted below, and the fact of the great post–World War II movement of blacks from the South to northern and midwestern cities leads to the inference that the term "migrants" was, in this case, a euphemism for blacks.

Told from the viewpoint of the city housing inspectors, not the migrants, the story began with the statement that "even if Chicago had 1,000 building inspectors, they could not prevent firetrap deaths originating in the mixture of bad housekeeping, liquor and a stove." The reporter added that the city could not solve the problems of a housing shortage made worse daily by an influx of migrants seeking "a promised land of big pay and easy pickings." The inspectors were quoted as saying, "Our problems begin in other states willing to supply carfare to unload their relief headaches on us." Out-of-state officials paint a glowing picture of Chicago, the inspectors claimed, "so migrants come with nothing but the shirts they're wearing." Mysteriously, they added, "Even a bird arranges a nest ahead of time."[3]

Given this picture of city officials resenting the influx of blacks into Chicago, and claiming them to be feckless, alcoholic, and slovenly, it is perhaps not surprising that the *Tribune* devoted such a large percentage of its coverage of blacks to crime news and ran a much smaller percentage of civil rights–related news in the 1950s than did the other papers.

During the 1960s the *Tribune*'s editorials showed strong hostility toward any persons or groups seeking a change in the status quo on racial matters, accusing them of being agitators, lawbreakers, the tools of Communist interests, or, at best, wrong-headed. An observation on the *Tribune*'s attitude toward civil rights demonstrators at Northwestern University was provided by two letters to the editor from about sixty journalism students at Northwestern. The students said the *Tribune*'s coverage of the demonstrations "hammered at the black student tactics and ignored the issues involved." These words echo exactly the finding of Thomas Kelly's study that the *Tribune* tried to discredit the proponents of racial change while completely avoiding consideration of the underlying injustices they were seeking to correct.

The students also claimed that the paper's editorial hostility toward the protesters had spilled over into the news coverage of the demonstrations, and they cited several examples. They criticized the

Tribune's news and editorial coverage of the events as distorted, shallow, and serving to "reinforce old prejudices, old stereotypes."

The *Tribune*'s apparent hostility toward blacks was, to some extent, reflected in the paper's coverage patterns in the 1960s. The paper gave much more emphasis than any of the other newspapers to crimes committed by blacks, as Table 1 shows. It also gave scant attention to white leaders' calls for integration, and about half of its total in the white resistance to integration subcategory was comprised of its own anti-integration editorials. Finally, the paper was the only one of the four that did not provide any coverage of black problems in the 1960s issues coded.

The *Tribune*'s coverage of blacks showed definite improvements during the 1970s. This newspaper was the only one whose coverage of stereotypical activities decreased, both in column inches and as a percentage of its total coverage of blacks, in the 1970s from what it had been in the 1960s. Black crime news accounted for only 6 percent of the *Tribune*'s 15 percent of coverage of stereotypical activities, marking a dramatic decrease in the *Tribune*'s attention to black crime from the two previous periods.

In addition, this paper ran the largest amount of coverage of black problems, as a proportion of its total coverage of blacks in the 1970s, of all the papers studied. This attention to black problems was a notable change for the *Tribune*, which had provided no coverage in this area in the issues coded for the two previous periods. As Figure 3 indicates, however, only 5 percent of this coverage concerned the problems of local blacks; this was the lowest percentage of local coverage provided by any of the newspapers.

Finally, the *Tribune* greatly increased its attention to blacks as part of the everyday life of the community in this period, although it should be noted that two out of every three *Tribune* items coded under everyday life seemed to be photos; the paper really provided very little actual information about the everyday activities of blacks.

All these changes seem to suggest some alteration in the *Tribune* management's attitude toward blacks during the 1970s. The earlier-mentioned editorial stance of the paper in the 1970s demonstrates this change but also indicates the editorial writers' continuing reluctance to see the status quo disturbed in order to redress social inequalities. Several editorials stressed the theme that segregation in housing and public schools in Chicago "stands solid, upheld by public opinion," and integration would be indefinitely deferred.

One of the paper's most positive editorial statements concerning school integration was made in an editorial criticizing the Boston mobs that demonstrated against school integration and pelted Senator Edward Kennedy with vegetables when he tried to speak at an anti-busing rally. "Busing a child into a totally unfamiliar and very likely inhospitable area," the editorial said, "isn't the best way to improve the quality of his education. But it's probably better than keeping a child out of school so that he can watch his mother hurl groceries at a U.S. senator."[4]

CONCLUDING OBSERVATIONS

Clearly, the four newspapers studied varied widely in their approach to coverage of black Americans, even though some similarities were evident in the amount and nature of their coverage during the three periods studied. It is evident that the amount of attention each newspaper paid to blacks changed over the three periods.

In the 1970s issues studied, all the papers seemed to exhibit changes in their approach to coverage of blacks, most notably in continuing to provide much higher levels of coverage than they had done before the years of the civil rights movement. In general, the papers focused on black problems and on blacks as part of the everyday life of the community and nation much more than they had in the two previous periods studied, and they did a better job of covering the causes of protest activities.

NOTES

1. Ralph McGill, *The South and the Southerner* (Boston: Little, Brown, 1963), p. 295. Thaddeus Stevens, a Pennsylvania congressman, was an abolitionist and a bitter critic of compromise measures with the South before the Civil War and of conciliation after.

2. Edwin Diamond, "The Agony of Responsibility," *Columbia Journalism Review* 13, no. 5 (Jan./Feb. 1975), 11, 13–14.

3. Gladys Priddy, "Asks Warning of Bad Housing for Migrants," *Chicago Tribune*, 7 Dec. 1950, Sec. 5, p. 1.

4. "The Mob Mentality Again," *Chicago Tribune*, 13 Sept. 1974, Sec. 1, p. 10.

CHAPTER 8

not report
strength

Recent Coverage Criticisms

As the ghetto riots died down and the confrontational events of the civil rights revolution subsided in the late 1960s, so did the urgency of journalists' attention to the quality of their coverage of American blacks and race relations. But the subject was by no means forgotten.

In the early 1970s, the University of Maryland's journalism department held a lecture series on improving communications in the inner city, and the Community Relations Service of the U.S. Justice Department was involved in numerous conferences on the news media and race relations. Later in the decade, mass media/minorities conferences were held at the University of Michigan, Boston University, and Fisk University, among others, and discussions of the situation of minorities in journalism were held at the conventions of the American Society of Newspaper Editors, the American Newspaper Publishers Association, and the Associated Press Managing Editors.

The focuses of the discussions at journalists' conferences had shifted slightly, however, from those of the media/race relations seminars held during the 1960s. Although the quality of media coverage of minorities was still a concern, discussions now centered around the media's hiring of minority journalists: whether the hiring was proceeding fast enough, what obstacles prevented more hiring and promotion of minority journalists, and problems these journalists experienced.

A similar concentration on minority journalists in the media was evident in the articles in periodicals for professional journalists during the 1970s. For every one article assessing the quality of media coverage of black Americans, the reader could find six measuring the media's performance in hiring minority journalists. The problems involved in training and placing minority journalists in the white media were the theme of several other meetings sponsored by the ASNE, which had adopted in 1978 the goal of having the same proportion of minorities employed in the nation's newsrooms by the year 2000 as are represented in the population at large.

It seems odd that so much of the attention of professional journalists was directed during the 1970s toward the hiring of minority journalists, because although this course was strongly recommended by the Kerner Commission and journalists during the previous decade, it was by no means the only suggestion advanced for improving coverage of minorities. A reader could almost come to the conclusion, from studying the professional journalism periodicals during the 1970s, that most media executives and journalists had unconsciously concluded that the media's deficiencies in minority coverage could be eliminated if the media could only hire enough minority reporters.

To some extent this assumption is correct; minority journalists can bring—and, indeed, have already brought—to their jobs a knowledge, sensitivity, and skill that have greatly enhanced their medium's coverage of minorities and coverage in general. But surely the whole burden of improving media coverage of minorities should not be placed on minority reporters. It seems obvious that such improvement also demands increased knowledge and sensitivity from white journalists as well. In addition, a recommitment to this project and a rethinking and reordering of traditional journalistic values and practices by media executives seems needed.

Despite journalists' preoccupation with the numbers game of minority hiring, various expressions of concern over the nature of media coverage of black Americans can be found in the journalism periodicals and conference reports of the 1970s. Many of these concerns, not surprisingly, were voiced by minority journalists themselves.

The very obvious strides the media has made in the past two decades in covering black Americans can be observed in the appearance of more black faces in newspapers and on television, much more coverage of blacks involved in everyday-life activities, dropping of the race label except when relevant, discontinuing of "colored news" sections, appearance of columns written by blacks, a greater sensitivity to black pride and black presence, and the greatly increased number of black journalists working in the white media. Despite these signs of progress, both black and white journalists who discussed media coverage of blacks in the 1970s and early 1980s seemed to take a somber tone. Uniformly they seemed to feel that racist attitudes and practices still permeated the media and that much remained to be done to tell the true story of the experience of black Americans.

COMMITMENT DIMINISHED

A theme underlying many of the reporters' remarks was the idea that white journalists and media executives seemed to feel, after the riots and civil rights movement died down, that America's racial crisis had been solved and that continued coverage of blacks and the issues affecting them was no longer of vital importance. Roger Wilkins of the *New York Times* suggested in 1975 that this progression began when, in the early 1970s, white fear of blacks diminished after it became clear that angry blacks were not going to burn down the cities or destroy the nation. He added that on racial issues the press seemed to have adopted a U.S. senator's advice on Viet Nam: "Declare victory and withdraw."

White America, he said, "having discovered the race problem in the sixties and finding it too hard," began forcing powerful distortions on reality in order to design new fantasies suitable for shunting the issue aside. The current fantasy, he wrote, focused on superficial improvements and held that, "despite the persistent high rates of black poverty, consistent failures to educate black children, rising crime rates and the steady erosion of the foundations of urban life . . . America has broken the back of its racial problem." He quoted a news executive who, disturbed by revelations of conditions in the black community, observed, "Black problems are practically invisible now. We don't see them anymore."[1]

Paul Good, in his book published in 1975, commented on this same erosion of concern among the media. The ghetto gets larger each day and deteriorates faster, he said, and other signs of black problems are obvious, but the media ignore them.[2]

Four years later, Thomas Noland illustrated another aspect of

white Americans' continuing ignorance of black concerns in his report of the difficulties white reporters in Decatur, Alabama, had in
understanding black protests over the arrest and trial of a black man
accused of raping a white woman. "Reporters, accustomed to thinking that the civil rights battle had been fought out years ago, barely
grasped the dimensions of the story," Noland wrote. He added that
ignorance of black society crippled the local newspaper's coverage
and noted that although the paper listed black allegations about
racism in the city, it neither evaluated nor investigated them but
instead parried the charges.

Later, interviewing the head of the local chapter of the Southern
Christian Leadership Conference (SCLC), a reporter asked, "What
is it that you people want? White people don't understand. They say
you are as free as anyone. They don't understand what you people
are asking for." Noland observed that the paper "continues to ignore
the root causes of black frustration and white reactions."[3]

PERCEPTIONS FILTERED

Another concern reiterated with great frequency by the journalists discussing racial coverage in the 1970s and early 1980s was
that white media executives consistently prevented the perceptions
and perspectives of minority reporters from appearing and, instead,
forced their stories to fit the white view of reality. Wilkins wrote
that black newspeople "were usually hindered in their efforts to tell
the story of America as they saw it because their work product was
filtered through the general racial fantasy locked in the minds of
white editors." He added:

Their editors were generally unfamiliar with all but the most noted black
experts and resource people. Thus, a whole segment of insight and perception has either been excluded from or devalued in the process of developing
information that shapes and informs news judgments. Black writers con-
tinually encounter white editors insistent upon reshaping their work and
their insights to accord with white preconceptions and values. . . . The
experience of blacks writing for white editors is sometimes like pitching a
ballgame being called by a cross-eyed umpire.[4]

During the early 1970s, journalist Dorothy Gilliam quoted a Chicago reporter who said there was "little opportunity for black report-

ers to deal in depth and detail with basic issues which affect black people. . . . By the time a story runs the gamut of white editors, he said, often it is 'laundered if not eliminated.' "[5]

Also in the early 1970s, Ben Holman of the Justice Department's Community Relations Service commented at the University of Maryland lecture series about the white media's distortion of reality. Observing that media executives still defended their coverage of racial news with the claim that the media simply hold a mirror up to the world, Holman said he felt a more accurate analogy would be that the media hold not a mirror but a telescope, which they focus on a small segment of the nation's social landscape. In the process, Holman said, "Usually minorities suffer from what lens buffs call spherical aberration—fuzziness around the edges."[6]

In the latter part of the 1970s the situation was similar, although minority journalists' complaints were centered less on white management's "laundering" of their work than on its reluctance to promote blacks to executive positions and to share power. "Even when all professional standards are met," Kotz wrote in 1979, "many white editors and publishers simply will not entrust basic news judgments to nonwhite professionals. White management is unwilling to place coverage decisions in the hands of people whose values and perspectives may differ from their own."[7]

One minority reporter observed in 1979, "What you find out very quickly is that newspapers play a tremendous role in shaping and influencing opinion in this country. Understand that, and then you know why the going is rough for those of us who manage to get in the door. Nobody wants Black folks this close to the throttle of this country."[8]

The story is the same in television, where in 1982 there were still no blacks or Hispanics among those most responsible for determining what goes on the air and how events are shown. As a result, according to Emery King of NBC, "There is no black input into decisions about stories affecting the lives of twenty million black people." One former CBS reporter noted that the lack of black news executives at CBS "often places a black reporter in the role of facing a hostile jury whose instincts and interests are totally different, based on their experiences, which are generally confined to the white mainstream."[9]

EVERYDAY-LIFE COVERAGE

The minority journalists' observations about media coverage of the black community since 1970 were that it remains both sketchy and negative. Kotz wrote in 1979 that the press "still does not report adequately the lives and aspirations of nonwhite Americans." He added that the New York newspapers "convey only the vaguest sense—except for crime news and a rare poverty story—of what actually happens in Brooklyn, Queens, the Bronx, and upper Manhattan." Black reporters in Atlanta, he said, echo a familiar charge of minority reporters, that the culture of their communities is ignored while leisure-time stories proliferate. In the West, Mexican-American and Asian reporters state that their communities are ignored or misrepresented.[10]

These criticisms were mentioned by many other journalists and were perhaps best summarized by the Reverend Jesse Jackson when he told an ANPA panel in 1979 that most blacks distrust the press because of "the four cardinal sins of the press." These are, Jackson said, that the press portrays blacks as less intelligent, less hard-working, more violent, and less universal than they really are.[11]

In 1979, Robert Maynard, who became one of the few black journalists to hold an executive position on a white newspaper, said, "What we are now seeking is portrayal of our communities as places inhabited by real people, not pathological fragments." He added that blacks were not asking that their communities be romanticized but that the media should report the health and creativity found there as well as the disease and crime.[12] Two years earlier, at the University of Michigan's Kerner Plus 10 conference, Maynard had said,

The whites have no notion on one hand of what it is like to live in today's inner city because our newspapers do so little to bring that fact alive. On the other hand, the positive aspects of black American history and culture are obscured for much the same reasons—because in all too many instances there is no black in a position to help shape a product so that it reflects accurately all the disparate elements that make up our society.[13]

A *Los Angeles Times* reporter said in 1979 that minorities in that city were not asking the *Times* to produce special-interest sections on the black and Chicano communities but simply "to consider their

interests in all issues worthy of coverage." What the minorities
sought, he said, was that "the paper fairly represent all points of
view in the community, and that it guard the interests of minorities
as zealously as it defends those of the dominant white community."[14]

The same idea was expressed at the 1985 ASNE conference by
Mervin Aubespin, president of the decade-old National Association
of Black Journalists. Stating that a newspaper's role was to present
various points of view and to portray all segments of the population,
Aubespin urged journalists to seek out black opinion on stories that
affect all citizens.[15]

It should be noted that these criticisms are not supported by the
findings of the empirical study reported in the preceding chapters.
The data in that project showed that the papers studied increased
their coverage of everyday-life activities of blacks and provided a
more evenhanded and representative portrayal of blacks. This discrepancy between the journalists' perceptions and the study's findings can be explained in several ways. Perhaps the increase in attention to blacks and the less-distorted coverage among the papers
studied were not typical of the press in general in the 1970s. Or
perhaps minority journalists felt that the coverage improvements
made were too limited—that even more space and increasingly representative coverage were needed.

STEREOTYPICAL COVERAGE

In 1972 Dorothy Gilliam reported several black leaders' charges
that the media perpetuated racism and stereotypes in its coverage of
blacks, and she quoted a Chicago journalist who said, "It's easier to
get a piece in on the Panthers or a street gang than on a block club or
community news."[16] His remarks seem to indicate that racial stereotypes still formed the grid through which news about blacks was
filtered.

Clinton Cox noted the same phenomenon four years later, when
he reported that in the New York press, "Blacks and Hispanics
commit crimes; their role as victims is slight. The victims are white.
And the closer they are to the middle-class status of the papers'
white editors, the bigger the story."

The statistics of the New York City Police Department, however, revealed a radically different picture, Cox wrote. According to the department's figures, half of the city's homicide victims were blacks and 30 percent were Hispanic; half of the victims lived in Harlem, East Harlem, or Bedford-Stuyvesant. "In the real homicide world," Cox wrote, "the average victim is a male who is black or Hispanic; two and one-half times as many black and Hispanic women are murdered as white women; white women comprise only one-half of one percent of all victims." The three New York papers' constant presentation of quite a different picture is, Cox wrote, "just one way the papers carefully structure (or rather, restructure) reality along racial lines comfortable to them."[17]

Cox presented a detailed analysis of how the papers gave considerable play to the murders of white youths from upper-class suburbs but ignored the equally brutal deaths of black children in poor sections of the city. The discrepancy in coverage was even more pronounced, he said, when the victims were killed by police. Coverage of a middle-class white youth shot by police focused heavily on witnesses' accounts of the killing and the boy's parents' claims against the police. But several months earlier, Cox said, when a black man was killed by police with nine shots, five of them in the back, the papers barely mentioned bystanders' versions of the incident and consistently presented the events in the words and viewpoint of the police. The papers also covered scantily, and only from police sources, black citizens' subsequent protests of this and similar incidents, Cox said, and they failed to follow up on the citizens' charges.[18]

Cox's observations are reminiscent of the 1968 Columbia University conference, where participants repeatedly stated that the media were partial toward police, consistently featured violence by blacks against the police, but played down police brutality against blacks.[19] These charges highlight a problem of media coverage of race relations that does not seem to have changed in the slightest in the past two decades—the media's ignoring of bad relations between the police and low-income black communities and their focusing almost exclusively on the police side of the story in any incident where "police brutality" is charged by blacks.

And yet this matter seems central to racial tension in America. The Kerner report indicated that a majority of the urban riots of the 1960s were sparked by an incident in which a black had been arrested, beaten, or killed by police, and most riots since then have been triggered by the same kind of occurrence.[20]

A vivid illustration of the black community's concern with this problem was provided in the University of Washington seminar report, which noted that although the meeting was set up to consider media-black relations, a considerable amount of time was spent discussing police-black relations. While the black participants were willing to discuss the media, the report stated, they felt such a strong animosity toward the police that the presence of newsmen was sufficient to unleash a flood of criticism against the police. The participants apparently were eager to inform reporters about their grievances concerning police behavior in the black community because they felt that if journalists became aware of this situation and exposed it to the reading public, some corrective measures might be taken. The report said,

> It was in their relations with the police, rather than the press, that the Black individuals appeared to believe their problems were greatest. Black speaker after Black speaker called upon newsmen to direct the media searchlight of truth upon alleged police misbehavior. It was there, that the pain was greatest. It was there, that the sores were rawest.[21]

The media, however, continue to ignore this problem. They also seem prone to present the police only as upholders of law and order, black victims as possibly deserving of their fate, and black witnesses as probably unreliable.

Observations by Claude Brown, author of *Manchild in the Promised Land*, suggest some possible reasons for the white media's myopia concerning relations between poor inner-city blacks and the police. Stating that in the ghetto "police corruption is more overt than in other environments," he notes,

> The residents of Black America are consistently subjected to the worst facets and behavior of the policeman. In the ghetto a policeman wields power. He is not the respectful and even humble public servant that he is in middle and upper class communities; he is often a tyrant.[22]

James Farmer of CORE, in his book on the civil rights movement, also comments on the vast difference between the middle-class white's view and experience of police and those of ghetto blacks. Of all the issues of his leadership career, he said, the one that was most incomprehensible to CORE's white liberal friends, and which caused a significant drop in contributions, was Farmer's stance on police abuses. Middle-class whites simply could not believe, he said, that the friendly man in blue who waved to them and helped their children across the street could be indiscriminantly brutal to blacks in the inner city. And yet, he notes, the *function* of police is most appreciated by ghetto dwellers, to whom "safety in the streets is the number-one concern."[23]

While it would be as unrealistic to consider all police villains as it is to consider them all heroes, these observations emphasize the need for the media to take a closer look at police relations with black communities in the inner city. Perhaps the media have failed to inquire deeply into this area because the truths that would emerge might prove uncomfortable to white middle-class society.

Hartmann and Husband relate several examples of the British press downplaying black protests against police harassment and instances of police failure to protect Pakistanis from racist assaults. The authors conclude that the media minimized these situations to maintain sociocultural consensus by not questioning the integrity of British police. Press reticence about the incidents also may have arisen, Hartmann and Husband suggest, from reporters' dependence upon the police for information about crime.[24]

Clinton Cox suggests another reason for distortions in media coverage of blacks, crime, and the police. Because of the New York papers' coverage, he said, he knew something about the personal qualities and aspirations of young white homicide victims, but nothing about the personal lives of murdered blacks, so the poor minority victims remained strangers to him, in death as in life. "The newspapers see to that," he said, "just as they see to it that photos of black and Hispanic criminals often stare out at me from the papers, and that stories about these criminals are more likely to be printed than stories about black and Hispanic victims." He concluded that the newspapers "constantly remind me in myriad ways that some lives are worth caring about and some are not."[25]

Some support for the journalists' claim that the media continue to perpetuate racial stereotypes, especially the image of the black criminal, was found in the empirical study reported in this book. Three of the four newspapers increased in column inches their coverage of antisocial actions committed by blacks. Emphasizing black crime news, failing to provide any counteracting coverage of other activities of blacks, and ignoring black victims may be a common practice among other newspapers across the nation.

In 1978 the Reverend Benjamin Hooks, director of the NAACP, pointed out once again the importance of the media's role in race relations. "Given the nature of our divided society," Hooks said, "the press becomes a major link between black and white communities. It can either reinforce prejudices, racial stereotyping and the status quo, or it can take on the role of broadening the horizons of its readers."[26]

EMPHASIS ON CONFLICT

The media's tendency to overplay conflict simply because of its dramatic value was mentioned by several journalists in the 1970s discussions of coverage, but it was not nearly as dominant a complaint then as it had been a decade earlier—perhaps because the 1970s produced fewer protests and riots to cover.

Two educators criticized the media's focus on violence over progress when they stated that the integration and social changes achieved in Mississippi in the late 1960s had gone largely unreported. They noted that in the early 1960s Mississippi was headlined regularly in the nation's newspapers because of racial violence there. Ten years later, the authors said, "a momentous social and educational change has taken place in the state, but because peaceful progress is not so newsworthy as confrontation and killing, this change has not received the attention it deserves."[27]

Their charge seems justified. Any improvements in race relations that have occurred in the South in the past decade have received little media attention. In fact, the whole racial situation in the South seems as seldom reported in the news media now as it was before the mid-1950s. What it is like to be black in the South is as much a mystery to white readers now as it was three decades ago.

The strict segregation of public facilities and the implacable hostility of many southern whites toward integration and toward blacks seeking civil rights were vividly illustrated by the media during the late 1950s and the 1960s. But since little information about the situation of blacks in the South has been provided by the media in the past decade, many whites have the impression that no problems remain. However, it is hard to believe that the deep-rooted prejudice that led to the ugly violence against civil rights workers of both races in the 1960s has been significantly eradicated in less than two decades.

How much progress on integrating schools has really been achieved in the Deep South? How much change has occurred in whites' attitudes toward blacks? What positive contributions to both races have resulted from the securing of greater civil rights for blacks in the South? These questions are long overdue for coverage by the media.

By the late 1960s the racial story had moved North, as reporters gathered to cover the conflicts surrounding school busing in cities there. Edwin Diamond observed in the mid-1970s, during Boston's school integration troubles, that when he compared his experience of Boston with the besieged city being reported by the national news media, he often wondered what city the media were describing. "I have the eerie sense of reacting the way Southerners must have reacted a decade ago when the liberal press came to cover the racial stories there," Diamond said.[28]

While incidents of violence and tension did occur as Boston's school integration began, Diamond stated, they were played up so much by reporters from outside the city that the picture those media presented was markedly distorted. He stated, "It was the usual hype—still, seven years after the Kerner Commission report." Diamond quoted a wire service journalist describing his news bureau's preoccupation with the conflict aspect of the situation. If a story went out of Boston with "classes were generally peaceful" in the lead, the reporter recalled, "the New York office would ask the bureau to move up the violence from the fifth or sixth paragraph; reporters soon got the message."[29]

Diamond's observations illustrate clearly that, despite all the coverage criticisms leveled at the media in the 1960s, a decade later American media executives were still unwilling to abandon their preoccupation with conflict, no matter how much their focus distorted reality for their audiences. It seems amazing that American journalism, which has become so much more responsible and powerful than it was in the sensationalistic, yellow journalism days of the turn of the century, should not have evolved its approach to reporting conflict much beyond that used over eighty years ago. Instead of attempting to present their audiences with an accurate picture of the mood and scale of an event, and perhaps exploring the reasons why the conflict occurred in the first place, media executives all too often seem to instruct reporters to exaggerate the nature of the violence in order to give the coverage more impact—even when that impact is misleading.

However, it should be noted that the newspapers studied in this project did do a much better job of covering the causes of racial conflict in the 1970s than they had in the issues sampled from the preceding decade, although this may not be a common practice among most newspapers. The papers studied also had provided coverage, although perhaps not enough of it, of instances of successful integration and interracial cooperation in both the 1960s and 1970s, so they did provide some good news about race relations.

The Boston school integration stories also indicate that journalists apparently were still covering the situations underlying the conflict sketchily. In an article written in 1976, Diamond observed, "The violence inside decaying, urban school systems is less easy to portray" than violence in the streets. Stating that many media were trying to do a better job in this area, he added, however, that "even the better news organizations still shrink from serious discussion of race and class in America." He noted that by the mid-1970s, when the rights of blacks seemed to clash with the rights of others, the "liberal consensus that supported the civil rights movement in the 1960s had broken down."[30]

Diamond's writings also underscore the news media's continued tendency to play up racial conflict in other cities while downplaying troubles in their own. He noted that during the first week of school in Boston, local papers ran photographs that illustrated the picture they were trying to convey, of an opening week that was largely calm, despite incidents of violence. Out-of-town media, however, were less concerned about "balance" and more concerned about the photos' impact, he said. Thus of the seventy-six school-related photos the two major Boston papers ran during the first week of school, only ten showed violence, while four out of the seven pictures run by the *New York Times* showed violent action, as did three of the *Washington Post*'s six photos.[31]

COVERAGE OF PROBLEMS

Journalists who discussed media coverage of minorities in the 1970s often reiterated the charge from the 1960s that the media failed to cover the problems of black Americans, especially those in the inner city. They also seemed to feel that the reason for this lack of coverage was the same as it had been before—white indifference.

Kotz wrote in 1979 that "the press still fails to report adequately the poverty, racism, and despair which bred the riots of the sixties."[32] During that same year, at a media/minorities conference at Boston University, another journalist stated that "few editors listened to pleas to cover simmering black America."[33]

In 1981, DeMott pointed out how the plight of black Americans living in the nation's central cities still was not reported except when disturbances occurred. He also suggested that since the beginning of the country's urban crisis coincided with that of the civil rights revolution, and because the problems of the inner city most severely affect blacks, many news people have been conditioned to read the word "urban" to mean "black." He says, "White racism has become a critical factor in the neglect of our cities, and the reluctance of some news people to involve themselves more deeply in the effort to explain today's urban crisis."[34]

A decade earlier, Ben Holman had expressed the same idea in the University of Maryland lecture series. He said that not enough media attention was given to the inner city's underlying problems. He added, "Furthermore, if the media are going to give these problems the proper attention, they must also concentrate on the white problem of institutional and individual racism, which is really the root cause of much of what prevails in black and brown communities."[35] A similar idea was presented in the same lecture series by *Milwaukee Journal* managing editor Joseph Shoquist, who said that the basic causes of race riots are not speeches by militants or incidents with police but are "the despair of the ghetto dweller and the failure of whites to comprehend and respond."[36]

These men's words underscore the conclusions drawn by Tom

Wicker of the *New York Times* in his introduction to the Kerner report thirteen years earlier. Stating that the commission concluded that white racism was the single overriding cause of the urban riots, Wicker said the essence of the commission's charge was "what white Americans have never fully understood—but what the Negro can never forget—is that white society is deeply implicated in the ghetto. White institutions created it, white institutions maintain it, and white society condones it."[37] The indications from the 1970s are that instead of changing the ghetto, white society is continuing to condone its existence.

One result of that condoning was described by Claude Brown when he wrote, "To a perturbing extent, ghettoes are factories where society manufactures delinquents who eventually evolve into full-fledged criminals and drug addicts."[38] The injustice and the huge waste of human potential inherent in this situation are obvious. Perhaps less obvious is that the white society indifferent to those living in the inner city also pays a toll for this state of affairs, both in the suffering of whites who are victimized by the criminals thus produced and in the costs of police protection and supporting courts and prisons to handle the criminals who are caught. In this area, as in so many other aspects of race relations, the white man's stake in equal justice and opportunity for all races is just as real as the black man's, but less easily noticed.

In 1975, Roger Wilkins had described the media's ignoring of the problems of the inner city black in the early years of the decade. Because speculations about another "long, hot summer" had begun to surface again in 1975, Wilkins said, editors were again becoming a little concerned about the temper of the black ghetto youth. He wrote, "Unemployed black youngsters were not a story when harsh urban life and unemployment were destroying their families, when the schools quit on them or when from ineptitude or insensitivity the country's social agencies were battering the spirit out of them." They were again becoming a story, Wilkins said, only when "their anger—unlike the destruction of everything positive in their lives—is perceived as relevant to the quality of American life."[39] His charge echoes that of Clinton Cox and many American blacks—to the media, some lives just are not worth caring about, unless they threaten the comfort or safety of white Americans.

Here again, it must be noted that all but one of the newspapers studied in this project devoted much more space to coverage of the problems facing black Americans in the 1970s issues sampled than they had in the previous decade, although this kind of coverage never rose higher than 13 percent of a paper's total coverage of blacks in the issues coded. Also, the problems of local black communities and the grievances of ghetto residents received little attention from the papers studied, during the 1970s. Other papers across the country may typically provide even less of these kinds of coverage.

RACISM IN THE MEDIA

Many of the journalists' charges about the media's coverage of minorities since 1970 are underlaid by the accusation of white racism. This racism, the reporters say, is manifested in only cursory attention to the black community, a focus on negative images of blacks and on conflict, and indifference to the despair of many urban blacks. But white indifference and hostility in the media can take other forms, too. Sometimes, even the way the media report and interpret social phenomena can be harmful.

For instance, DeMott noted in 1981 that the media had been giving considerable coverage to openly racist bigots and hate groups in the previous few years. The media attention to these groups was so extensive, DeMott said, that the Student Christian Leadership Conference (SCLC) president had observed that "mass communications, which used to be dependable allies in the struggle for human rights, may be adversaries today."

DeMott also noted the media's failure to explore the causes and possible solutions to the urban crisis and their failure to interpret affirmative action. "One of the greatest challenges encountered by America's press in the decade following the Kerner Commission inquiry was its interpretation of affirmative action programs," he wrote. "By allowing opponents of affirmative action to brand it 'reverse discrimination,' the news media failed in many ways to explain it properly."

DeMott quoted Carl Stokes as saying, during the controversy over the Allan Bakke lawsuit, that "the media, finding 'reverse discrimination' a handy phrase to describe a complex issue, uses the phrase repeatedly." In doing so, DeMott indicated, the media had oversimplified and misrepresented a highly complex issue and helped subvert affirmative action programs.

"What would be the effect," Stokes inquired, "of news reports showing the extent to which children of alumni, athletes, musicians and residents of distant states are given priority admission to universities?" He said the media had an obligation to report the issue of minority admissions and affirmative action in the context of the civil rights advances made and not made.[40]

Stokes had a good point. Critics of affirmative action in admissions did not seem to mind that America's elite always get priority admission to universities; only when minorities were favored in the admissions process did cries of protest arise. The situation is reminiscent of the middle-class whites who complained throughout the 1970s and early 1980s about ghetto blacks whom the whites felt they were supporting on welfare. The whites did not seem to care, or perhaps had not been made aware, that less than 7 percent of their federal tax dollars went to welfare, while about 60 percent went to military-related spending. The fat budgets, the rich perquisites, the gross waste and mismanagement, and the "fat cats" were in the military, not on welfare.

MINORITY HIRING

During the late 1960s and early 1970s scores of programs to train and hire more minority journalists were initiated. Many of them were established by educational institutions like Columbia University, others were initiated by news organizations, and many were partly subsidized by bodies such as the Ford Foundation and the Gannett Fund. The programs included summer programs for training minority journalists, special undergraduate and graduate degree programs, scholarships, on-the-job training, and internships.

The ASNE and ANPA, as well as other professional and educational organizations like the National Conference of Editorial Writers, the National Association of Black Journalists, and the Association for Education in Journalism and Mass Communication, also initiated efforts to encourage the hiring and promotion of minority journalists. The Institute for Journalism Education established JOB/NET, a national clearinghouse linking minority journalists and daily newspapers, and the Gannett and Knight-Ridder newspaper chains set up aggressive affirmative action programs.

All these efforts have produced some significant results. Employment of minorities in the media rose from less than 1 percent in

1972 to 5.5 percent in 1982, and these journalists already have made an important contribution to the media. They have pushed for more adequate coverage of minority communities; kept alive the issue of the quality of the media's coverage of black Americans; supported programs to train, hire, and promote more minority journalists; risen to positions as columnists and editors, and in many cases have upgraded their medium's coverage and prestige.

This is the positive side of the picture. On the negative side are the facts that minorities in the media still represent only one-third of their proportion in the general population, the unemployment rate of black journalism graduates is twice as high as that of white journalism graduates, almost two-thirds of the nation's newspapers employ no minorities, and of the 2,700 minority journalists in the newspaper business, only a few score hold newsroom jobs of real power.

The situation is the same in television. The U.S. Commission on Civil Rights, in its 1977 report entitled *Window Dressing on the Set*, stated that minorities were almost totally excluded from decision-making positions at local stations. By late 1982 only 9 of the nation's 800 commercial television stations had black executives, and only six of the three television networks' 500 vice presidents were members of a minority group—and none was in a news division.[41]

Several minority reporters at the 1977 University of Michigan conference noted that a news organization's coverage of minorities is not much affected by the number of minority journalists it employs if none of these journalists hold executive positions in which they can affect decisions about which stories are to be covered and how they are to be presented. Because so few minority reporters who entered the media in the early 1970s have been promoted to middle-management jobs, the participants said, many of them became frustrated and left journalism, and bright journalism students realize they will have little opportunity to move to the top.[42]

Many journalists have observed that media executives' interest in hiring minority journalists has faded just like their interest in covering black America. In 1979, Kotz reported a definite backlash in journalism, as in other fields, from "those who feel threatened by any semblance of affirmative action." He noted that in a highly competitive job market, the rights of women and minorities often clash, and some editors find it easier to hire or promote a woman.

Kotz also noted that "many industry leaders no longer recognize an obligation to redress the racism of the past" and that several programs for training minority journalists had been closed down.[43] Kotz's sense that media executives had a diminishing commitment to hire minority journalists was borne out by an 1982 ASNE Minorities Committee report, which stated, "The rate of progress in integrating newspaper staffs has declined consistently and increasingly during each of the last five years."[44] That same year, an ABC journalist said of minority employment in television, "The climate in the country has changed. Not only isn't there any pressure to promote blacks—I see an erosion of progress. They just don't care any more."[45]

The 1982 ASNE Minorities Committee report included the reasons given by some newspaper executives for their reluctance to hire minority reporters. Among their rationales were the ideas that if minority reporters were hired other staff members might resent them, people in the community might not accept them, and their hiring would lead to "suspicions among the higher echelons that we are becoming subversive."[46] According to minority journalists already employed in the media, none of these possible situations has materialized as a serious problem for them. But one fear mentioned by the editors surveyed by the ASNE has affected them strongly— the editors' belief that hiring minority reporters would mean temporarily reducing newsroom standards.

Time magazine reported in 1982 that many minority journalists feel that if their performance is not extraordinary, they are considered inferior. Although white reporters who are competent but not brilliant are accepted, many minority reporters feel that for them no such middle ground exists. *Time* quoted a black assistant news editor who said, "I have always felt that blacks had to prove themselves daily and give 110%, or be regarded as lazy, though a white colleague is not."[47]

Despite fine and even award-winning performances by many black journalists in the past fifteen years, the tired "lowering newsroom standards" shibboleth was raised once again when the Janet Cooke scandal broke. Amazingly, the *Wall Street Journal* suggested that Cooke's "Jimmy" hoax raised once more the "troublesome issues" of affirmative action.[48]

Another problem faced by minority journalists is the one described earlier in this chapter—winning the trust of their editors. Black journalists often mentioned during the 1970s and early 1980s that editors did not believe they would be objective in covering sensitive black-related stories and did not trust their perspectives. An example was Jesse Jackson's 1984 presidential campaign. Black journalists covering the campaign were in a difficult position from the beginning, several reporters observed, because of the difference between their perceptions of Jackson's campaign and their white media's initial refusal to take his campaign seriously and, in some cases, their antipathy toward Jackson. Later, as the entourage covering Jackson became larger and whiter, black reporters were faced with different loyalty tests.[49] The most controversial of these was Milton Coleman's role in reporting Jackson's "Hymietown" remarks.

Thus, although the media have made great improvements in newsroom integration, real equality of opportunity has not yet been achieved. The news media remain one of the most segregated American institutions, hiring has leveled off, promotion of minority reporters is seldom achieved, and minority perspectives are distrusted.

SCHOLARLY STUDIES

Few scholarly studies of media coverage of American blacks have been reported since 1970, and their findings do not present a uniform or comprehensive picture. In a few of the studies, however, it is possible to trace some familiar themes—black invisibility, media overreliance upon official sources, exclusion of black viewpoints, and less favorable display and treatment of items about blacks than is given to items about whites in comparable circumstances.

In 1971, Guido Stempel III reported on his study of the visibility of blacks in news and news-picture magazines. He had studied the pictures in news-editorial and advertising content in five major news and news-picture magazines for the first ten weeks of 1960 and 1970, and he found that, in 1960, 95 percent of the news pictures and 99 percent of the ad pictures showed whites only, while in 1970 these percentages had dropped to 87 percent of the news pictures and 97 percent of the ads. Thus, the reader of these magazines in 1970 saw nine or ten pictures of whites only for every one showing blacks only or whites and blacks together.[50]

Richard Pride and Daniel Clarke sampled television newscasts concerning race issues between August of 1968 and April of 1970 and concluded the broadcasts sampled did not seem to bear out blacks' allegations that the media supported white authorities and police against blacks. The researchers found that black militants and white racists were treated very negatively in the newscasts, while both blacks and the police received about equal amounts of positive and negative treatment.[51]

After the May 1970 killings at Jackson, Mississippi, State College, Edwin Williams analyzed the *Jackson Clarion-Ledger*'s coverage of the event and its aftermath. He found that the newspaper became the vehicle for the presentation of the police version of the incident, while all other viewpoints were excluded. For example, half of the column inches in the original story came from police, one-third from the mayor and governor, and only one-tenth from witnesses and the college community. Nowhere in the stories written by *Ledger* reporters, said Williams, was there a hint that many eyewitnesses disputed the police story that they fired only in response to sniper fire.

The paper also carried AP coverage of black community protests of the shooting but never covered a meeting of blacks or interviewed a black student, Williams said. He contrasted the distorted picture presented by the *Ledger* and its exclusion of black viewpoints with the much different coverage by the *Memphis Commercial Appeal*, the *New Orleans Times-Picayune*, and the wire services. Williams said he believed the *Ledger* covered the situation this way because the paper's owners were deeply entrenched in the Mississippi power structure and consistently insured that the paper avoided criticizing state and local government.[52]

Churchill Roberts studied coverage of blacks by television network newscasts and found that blacks appeared in 23 percent of the news segments and were heard in only one-third of these segments. In a study of coverage of black public officials during political campaigns in the daily newspapers of nineteen major cities between 1970 and 1977, Anju Chaudhary found that, although the stories on black elected officials were slightly longer than those on white politicians, the articles were slightly less favorably displayed and their content was less positive.[53]

In 1982, Mary Alice Sentman reported the results of her study of coverage of black Americans in *Life* magazine in selected years between 1937 and 1972, and her findings were noticeably similar to those of the research reported in the previous chapters of this book. She found that in 1967 and 1972, the last two years of the eight years sampled, coverage of black Americans increased sharply as a percentage of the magazine's total content. However, she said that despite this increase, "coverage of black America constituted a minute portion of *Life*'s content," with the highest level of coverage reaching less than 3 percent of the total. Of this share, she added, the bulk of the coverage featured black Americans who had become prominent through politics, entertainment, sports, or social protest activities. Coverage of the everyday-life activities of black Americans was "markedly absent" from the magazine in the years sampled, she noted.[54]

It seems clear that the research by communications scholars does not indicate that the media made any notable or dramatic changes in their coverage of black Americans during the late 1960s and 1970s. On the other hand, except for the Jackson paper's coverage, none of the media exhibited the blatant misrepresentations and racial bias shown in coverage studies from the first half of the century.

SUMMARY

Like the study of coverage described in this book, the other systematic analyses of coverage and discussions of journalists themselves indicate that the media have made some significant improvements in their coverage of black Americans. But at least as many more improvements remain to be made.

The upheavals of the 1960s apparently sensitized numerous journalists toward black Americans, and many of the obvious signs of stereotypical coverage have disappeared. At the same time, however, these tired stereotypes still seem to influence media executives to ignore black ghettos, except to cover crime in these areas; the black victims, and the conditions that spawn the crime, seem to remain unworthy of coverage in the eyes of media executives. In addition, journalists still seem reliant upon police sources and unwilling to present the views of blacks in cases where police brutality against blacks is charged.

The media's manner of reporting interracial conflicts illustrates clearly the media's need for continued improvement in their coverage of blacks—and, indeed, in their coverage of confrontations in general. Media executives seem positively wedded to a focus on violence, despite all the 1960s discussions indicating that such a focus presents the public with a distorted picture of the situation and is actively harmful to relations between the races. In this matter, media executives seem firmly stuck in the days of yellow journalism. Some executives' unwillingness to direct reporters to dig below the surface of the confrontations and explore the underlying causes distorts the picture they present to the public and heightens whites' fear of blacks, as it did in the 1960s.

Newspapers seem to be doing a better job than they did two decades ago in reporting the problems confronting black Americans. Yet now that blacks' dissatisfaction is no longer being expressed in forms that involve violence, media executives have lost any sense of urgency about exploring the nation's racial situation, minority journalists say. The perception of black Americans is that little has really changed since the 1960s, but white media audiences are being encouraged to think that most problems of blacks have been solved by the advances secured during the civil rights movement. In particular, the media seem reluctant to explore the whole thorny problem of the ghetto and the racism and economic system that created and maintains it. Black inner-city neighborhoods continue to remain a kind of no man's land to the American media.

Finally, the events of the 1960s seem to have produced among many white journalists and media executives a heightened consciousness that largely prevents manifestations of the more overt signs of white condescension and antipathy in the media. What seems to prevail, however, is an "us-them" kind of mentality, a notion that white America has done all that could reasonably be expected of it and a consequent unwillingness to explore thoughtfully the complex problems remaining and possible solutions to them.

In the area of hiring minority journalists, many media executives, newspaper chains, and professional organizations have done a fine job in bringing minority journalists into the media. On the other hand, however, hiring of minority reporters has fallen off, as has many executives' commitment to hire minorities. Clearly, a renewed effort is needed if the hiring and promotion of minority journalists is to approach significant levels and help eradicate racism from the media's coverage of black Americans.

Society would be greatly benefited if the media would recommit themselves to meeting these challenges. Black Americans and society in general have a right to expect from the media continued efforts to improve the inadequacies remaining in their coverage and employment of blacks. As the Kerner Commission stated, "A society that values and relies on a free press as intensely as ours, is entitled to demand in return responsibility from the press and conscientious attention by the press to its own deficiencies."[55]

NOTES

1. Roger Wilkins, "Further More: From Silence to Silence," *MORE*, July 1975, p. 27.

2. Good, p. 249.

3. Thomas Noland, "Old News from the New South," *Columbia Journalism Review* 18, no. 1 (May/June 1979), 41.

4. Wilkins, p. 27.

5. Dorothy Gilliam, "What Do Black Journalists Want?" *Columbia Journalism Review* 11, no. 1 (May/June 1972), 50.

6. Benjamin F. Holman, "How Can the Federal Government Facilitate Communication Within the City?" in Midura, ed., *Why Aren't We Getting Through? The Urban Communication Crisis* (Washington, D.C.: Acropolis Books, 1971), p. 107.

7. Nick Kotz, "The Minority Struggle for a Place in the Newsroom," *Columbia Journalism Review* 17, no. 6 (March-April 1979), p. 27.

8. DeWayne Wickham, "For Blacks on Daily Newspapers: The Same Old Song," *Black Enterprise*, Feb. 1979, p. 45.

9. Massing, pp. 39–40.

10. Kotz, "Minority Struggle," p. 24.

11. John Consoli, "Why Blacks Distrust the Press," *Editor & Publisher*, 28 April 1979, p. 87.

12. Kotz, "Minority Struggle," p. 28.

13. Marion Marzolf and Melba Tolliver, *Kerner Plus 10: Minorities and the Media: A Conference Report* (Ann Arbor: Univ. of Michigan Press, 1977), p. 3.

14. Felix Gutierrez and Clint C. Wilson II, "The Demographic Dilemma," *Columbia Journalism Review* 17, no. 5 (Jan./Feb. 1979), 55.

15. Mervin Aubespin, speech during Viewer Call-In program, ASNE annual meeting, Washington, D.C., April 12, 1985.

16. Gilliam, p. 50.

17. Clinton Cox, "Meanwhile in Bedford-Stuyvesant . . . ," *MORE*, Aug. 1976, p. 18.

18. Ibid., pp. 18–20.

19. *Conference on Mass Media and Race Relations*, p. 4.

20. *National Advisory Commission*, pp. 40, 120.

21. Schneider, *The Newsman and the Race Story*, p. 17.

22. Claude Brown, "The Ghetto View of Crime," *Race Relations Reporter*, Nov. 1974, p. 18.

23. James Farmer, *Lay Bare the Heart: An Autobiography of the Civil Rights Movement* (New York: Arbor House, 1985), p. 284.

24. Hartmann and Husband, p. 174.

25. Cox, p. 21.

26. DeMott, p. 10.

27. Vivian Horn and Mary Young, "The News These Days from Carthage, Mississippi," *Columbia Journalism Review* 13, no. 5 (Jan./Feb. 1975), 17.

28. Diamond, *The Agony of Responsibility*, p. 9.

29. Ibid., pp. 10–11.

30. Edwin Diamond, "School Busing: A Story in Two Acts," *Columbia Journalism Review* 14, no. 6 (March/April 1976), 36.

31. Diamond, "School Busing," p. 37.

32. Kotz, "Minority Struggle," p. 24.

33. Bill Kirtz, "Coverage of Minorities and Hiring Improves," *Editor & Publisher*, 1 Dec. 1979, p. 17.

34. DeMott, pp. 8–9.

35. Holman, p. 109.

36. Joseph W. Shoquist, "The Role of the Press in a Continuing Urban Crisis," in Midura, *Why Aren't We Getting Through?* p. 52.

37. Tom Wicker, "Introduction," in *National Advisory Commission*, p. vii.

38. Brown, p. 18.

39. Wilkins, pp. 27, 23.

40. DeMott, pp. 7, 10.

41. Massing, p. 38.

42. Marzolf and Tolliver, pp. 3–4, 8, 19–21.

43. Kotz, "Minority Struggle," pp. 24, 31.

44. Moreland, p. 6.

45. Massing, p. 44.

46. Moreland, pp. 6–7.

47. Henry, p. 90.

48. Les Payne, "Black Reporters, White Press—and the Jackson Campaign," *Columbia Journalism Review* 23, no. 2 (July/Aug. 1984), p. 32.

49. Ibid., pp. 33–36.

50. Guido Stempel III, "Visibility of Blacks in News and News-Picture Magazines," *Journalism Quarterly* 48, no. 2 (Summer 1971), 338–39.

51. Richard A. Pride and Daniel H. Clarke, "Race Relations in TV News: A Content Analysis of the Networks," *Journalism Quarterly* 50, no. 2 (Summer 1973), 328.

52. Edwin N. Williams, "Dimout in Jackson," *Columbia Journalism Review* 9, no. 2 (Summer 1970), 56–57.

53. Churchill Roberts, "The Presentation of Blacks on Television Network Newscasts," *Journalism Quarterly* 52, no. 1 (Spring 1975), 51–53; Anju G. Chaudhary, "Press Portrayal of Black Officials," *Journalism Quarterly* 57, no. 4 (Winter 1980), 641.

54. Mary Alice Sentman, "Black and White: Disparity in Coverage by Life Magazine from 1937 to 1972," *Journalism Quarterly* 60, no. 3 (Autumn 1982), 508.

55. *National Advisory Commission*, p. 367.

CHAPTER 9

Coverage Improvement
Suggestions

Many techniques for achieving better coverage of black Americans and racial issues may be inferred from the discussions in the previous chapters. But participants at the 1960s and 1970s conferences made some additional suggestions, many of them extremely creative, for methods journalists could use to achieve the goal of improved coverage. None of these involve a denial of the traditional objectives of journalism, although some would require a readjustment of reporters' perspective.

The suggestions presented here are divided in four parts. The first section includes proposals to prevent the coverage flaws arising from standard news values and news-gathering practices, such as those discussed in chapter 3. The second section proposes ways of avoiding the kinds of weaknesses caused by journalists' failure to fulfill their own standards of good reporting, as were examined in chapter 4. In the third section, a pilot project for opening channels of communication between the media and blacks is described, while suggestions for ways to improve hiring and training of minority journalists are reported in the final part of the chapter.

RETHINKING NEWS VALUES

Some of the most intriguing suggestions for improving coverage of race relations involve reevaluating traditional news values and news-gathering practices. These include journalists' conception of news as discrete events, their belief in the inevitable news value of conflict, their devotion to the ideal of objectivity, their tendency to rely on official sources, and the practice of jack-of-all-trades journalism. The suggestions point up some of the deepest weaknesses in American journalism as it is currently practiced and offer a slightly altered perspective on long-established beliefs about reporting.

In reference to the accepted notion of news as events, Caryl Rivers says that editors and reporters are going to have to understand that their usual definition of news is too narrow; they should realize, she says, that what does *not* happen is sometimes as newsworthy as what does. It requires more effort and initiative, she indicates, "to poke around and find out, for example, why the juvenile justice system is not working, than it does to rush out and cover a riot." Yet this kind of investigative reporting is urgently needed. She writes,

> It's not good enough to sit back and wait for the ghettos to burn or for people to hit the streets. They [journalists] will have to learn to be as aggressive in their coverage of issues that affect disenfranchised groups as they are in digging up political scandal or racing to five-alarm fires. This means a serious rethinking of some of the axioms they have accepted for years, about what is news and who is newsworthy.[1]

A similar notion of the importance of non-events was mentioned at the Columbia conference, where participants urged that the media should more closely scrutinize government programs to assess how well they are serving the people they are intended to help and that the media should point out when "the right thing is being done in the wrong place—for example, when job programs are conducted in areas where there are no appropriate job openings."[2]

If an editor is knowledgeable enough to recognize—and assign reporters to cover—the impact of negative developments and issues that concern minorities, it should be only a short step further to exploring situations, such as the quality of education or health care available to the poor or the problems of tokenism in hiring. In addition, as Rivers also has pointed out, editors need to follow up on yesterday's stories.[3] For example, what are the local black community's relations with the police? What is the mood of black ghetto youths? How has integration affected both black and white school children?

Another journalistic tradition overdue for reexamination is the media's emphasis on controversy. At the University of Washington seminar, Lawrence Schneider attacked journalists' conception of the news value of conflict and said this belief was a bias among members of the press. He stated that reporting conflict is not the only way to tell the story of man's relationship to man; instead, he said, "it is merely a particular historical and philosophical approach to the story of man which newspapers have embraced."[4]

His words raise numerous intriguing possibilities. For instance, conflict may well be the most dramatic manifestation of relations between people, but perhaps it is not the most important, or the most accurate, reflection of reality. Journalists willing to reexamine their assumption of the news value of conflict might come to feel that they can convey a more realistic picture of race relations by focusing on other aspects of the situation: black frustration and anger, white indifference, the advantages accruing to both races from cooperative interracial efforts. Perhaps signs of progress and evidence of cooperation might come to be considered as important as conflict in telling the racial story.

This idea was suggested at the Washington seminar, where "newsmen were urged to create a news value which places cooperation between individuals at least on a par with conflict between individuals."[5] A similar thought was mentioned at the Columbia conference, where participants said that journalists need to rethink their ideas about which topics are worthy of news coverage and should realize that human rights are perhaps the most important story of the day. News about basic human needs, they felt, is more important than stories about new autos, or political scandals, or other such subjects.[6]

Participants at the Washington conference had a lot to say about another sacred journalistic tradition—journalists' devotion to objectivity. In fact, the participants strongly urged an end to objective reporting on racial matters. Participant Edward Morgan called instead for an aggressive, anticipatory style of journalism that does not simply react to events but instead identifies important problems and begins to work on them. Rather than waiting for something to happen, he said, the press should be "investigating and finding out why it's going to happen, and trying to prevent it from happening if it's a Watts."[7]

At the same conference, Schneider recommended that journalists move from objective reporting of the race story to "commitment— vocally and clearly stated—to the goal of building a healthy, integrated society." Ben Holman said the black participants felt it was

up to the news media to take the initiative to try to understand what
is going on and what is needed in the black community and to
convey to white Americans that it was they who must take steps
toward securing justice for all Americans. "I think the media have a
tremendous obligation to try to impress on our White people that
until there is justice for minorities, regardless of their hue, this
country indeed will face many, many years of turmoil," Holman
said.[8]

A theme running through the entire conference was that the traditional standards of objectivity had produced poor coverage of the
racial story and that objectivity should be replaced by an energetic
dedication to coverage that would help create a more just and
healthy society.

British journalist Harold Evans believes that real objectivity requires a positive commitment to seek it. For example, he said, when
a news source distorts the truth, the reporter has the responsibility
to include—*in the story*—what the truth is, if it can possibly be
obtained.

Evans notes that American journalists are reluctant to mix fact
and comment in news stories, but he observes that this reluctance
helped Senator Joe McCarthy achieve the influence he did and that
it will always be helpful to the demagogue. "The Press has no duty
to print lies and distortions unchallenged," Evans writes. "So long as
it is clear what is fact and what is interpretation we have not merely
a right but a duty to keep the record straight."[9]

The same idea was discussed by Sylvan Meyer in his analysis of
southern press performance during the school desegregation conflict
of the second half of the 1950s. During the McCarthy era, Meyer
said, the press eventually realized that "it had the role of cross-
examiner and fact-checker, and that it had been derelict in rationaliz-
ing prominent use of his charges by noting that 'it is true that he said
it, whether what he said is true or not.'" The South's McCarthys
also took advantage of the media's willingness to report controversial
statements without checking, until the press once again ceased simply to report oratory and began seeking out the truth, Meyer
indicated.[10]

Evans says that when British newspapers print without checking
charges of terrible behavior by immigrants made by a vocal anti-
immigration British politician, the press is failing in its respon-

sibilities. "In such situations," he writes, "we are not much above the editors of the venomous sheets which spark the violence in India; our motives may not be malevolent, but the effect is identical." He adds that what he is suggesting is not really a departure from journalistic norms. Checking facts and trying to achieve accuracy is a customary task of journalists, he says; for this reason it is all the more odd that potentially damaging allegations are printed so casually, without any attempt to ascertain their accuracy.[11]

Another British journalist, Hugo Young, states, "The desirable commitment is simply a commitment to good race relations—a *positive* acknowledgement that racial coverage can directly affect race relations, and a *positive* determination to avoid unnecessary damage."[12]

The need to be especially careful in checking facts and in rigorously seeking the truth because of the sensitive nature of the racial story also was noted by the Kerner Commission. Stating that much of the 1960s riot coverage exaggerated both the mood and the extent of the riots, the commission said one reason for this distortion was the media's overreliance upon official sources who were themselves inexperienced in dealing with such disturbances and tended to overestimate damages.

"Reporters uncritically accepted, and editors uncritically published, the inflated figures," the commission stated, "leaving an indelible impression of damage up to more than ten times greater than actually occurred." The commission added that "to live up to their own professed standards, the media simply must exercise a higher degree of care and a greater level of sophistication than they have yet shown" in riot reporting. It noted that "many of the inaccuracies of fact, tone and mood were due to the failures of reporters and editors to ask tough enough questions about official reports, and to apply the most rigorous standards possible in evaluating and presenting the news."[13]

Journalists' reliance upon official sources is another familiar reporters' practice that should be altered, according to several conference participants. They suggested that reporters' need to find an official spokesperson may be the reason behind the much-discussed problem of the media's constantly seeking and even creating "Negro leaders" during the 1960s.

Numerous black seminar participants pointed out how unrealistic members of the press were to expect that one person could be a spokesperson for an entire black community, or even a segment of it, like black teenagers or black ministers. No reporter would expect such unanimity of opinion among similar segments of white society, they noted; why should they require it of blacks?

The right way to cover black America, conference participants felt, was not for the media to establish contact with a few black leaders and expect them to speak for the whole black population. Instead, at all the conferences, speaker after speaker stressed the need for reporters to cover the black communities in their areas regularly, to develop contacts among various groups and segments of black society, and to expose themselves to many different perspectives among blacks.

In several of the seminars, participants emphasized that reporters covering the ghetto should talk with the poorest and most desperate residents, not just the respectable establishment "leaders." Journalists were told that they should also try to understand the viewpoints of the dope addict, the prostitute, and the jobless youth on the street, because these people could provide them with important insights. One participant said, "You have got to communicate with the lowest guy in the gutter, the prostitutes on the street. You have to consult effectively with the Black community, and I don't mean inviting in 30 preachers for tea and crumpets."[14]

Philip Heisler, managing editor of the *Baltimore Evening Sun*, said at the University of Maryland lecture series that when his paper began trying to cover the inner city as it should be covered, reporters no longer covered only the NAACP, Urban League, and CORE but established contacts with the Black Panthers, Black Muslims, and dozens of other organizations. "Inner city reporters," he said, "have gotten to know and talk with the welfare recipients as well as the welfare director, the policeman on the beat as well as the district captain, the school kids as well as the principal, the pool hall operators as well as the swimming pool owners. And yes, even a dope peddler or two."[15]

Ben Bagdikian observed that in reporting the causes of the urban crisis, "journalism must not depend alone on official voices, who are even less aware of the dynamics of the ghetto than are journalists." He added that the ghetto has special communications and power problems and said reporters must "seek out the voiceless in the ghetto, not alone out of sympathy, but because this is the area of the most dangerous maladjustment in our political system and it is precisely the area that is least able to make itself known."[16]

Participants at the Columbia conference also had several suggestions in this area. In order to understand what is happening in the black community, reporters should listen carefully to all viewpoints, they said, adding that the reporter must be experienced enough to assess the different spokespersons and groups and be able to distinguish reliable informants from others. They warned that a leader should not be dismissed as insignificant because his or her organized following is small, since he or she may in fact express viewpoints that are held by masses of black people. They also called for more complete reporting of all serious black opinions, including those distasteful to whites.[17]

Caryl Rivers noted that journalists need to broaden their ideas about who is a reliable source. She cited as an example a reporter who was arranging a public affairs show on the problem of airport noise in suburban communities. The reporter wanted to use a working-class suburban housewife who had made herself knowledgeable about the problem, Rivers noted, and who had helped organize neighborhoods to resist the spread of a large urban airport. The show's producer, however, wanted to bring in an expert from MIT. The media executive's reluctance to accept the person who was really the most qualified to address that particular situation was "a clear example of the class bias common in the news business," Rivers said.[18]

Another long-standing journalistic practice overdue for reexamination is the jack-of-all-trades approach to reporting. This is the practice of sending reporters to cover events and situations about which they have very little background and inadequate opportunity to familiarize themselves before they must write the story.

One of the most challenging—and frustrating—aspects of a reporter's job is the frequent experience of being sent out to cover a story about which he or she knows nothing except the information acquired from a hasty reading of the newspaper's previous stories on the subject. Every reporter has more than once found himself or herself covering a meeting at which he or she was unfamiliar with the principal speakers, ignorant of the group's past actions, and unaware of the issues being fought out below the surface.

Fortunately, most reporters are intelligent and highly curious people who will try, in the situation just described, to counteract their own ignorance by asking innumerable questions and doing more research in the newspaper's morgue before they have to write their story. But the situation is fraught with opportunities for reporters to misinterpret what they saw and heard or to miss the significance of something that happened.

Media executives try, as much as possible, to prevent these kinds of problems by assigning reporters to beats, where they constantly deal with the same organizations and people and thus develop background knowledge, contacts, and expertise and can judge the day's events in some kind of perspective. The same advantages are obtained by hiring experts in certain fields, such as science or business or politics. A point made at several of the conferences was that the media should also hire experts in black life and concerns and interracial relationships.

In the UCLA conference report, Jack Lyle stated that many news executives were realizing that an objective news report can be more biased than an interpretative one. Thus, they were hoping to train specialized writers who could bring to an event a background of expertise and who also could report the event with some kind of historical perspective.[19] Conference participants believed this particular kind of expert was needed by the media in reporting events and situations concerning blacks and black-white relations.

At the UCLA conference Beverlee Bruce said she found it ludicrous that although the media could find and employ foreign correspondents who were knowledgeable about the countries to which they were assigned, the media did not have any experts on blacks in America. A Los Angeles journalist agreed and called for the hiring of black reporters who were specialists in race reporting. "After all," he said, "we have police reporters, aviation editors, science editors; why not have Negro editors?"[20]

At all the conferences lively discussion centered on the question of whether minority reporters should be automatically assigned to cover minority affairs. Many speakers of both races felt this was a kind of segregation and even racial stereotyping—to force a black reporter to cover the black community whether he or she wants that assignment or not, or to assume that a black middle-class college graduate, for example, is best qualified, because of his or her skin color, to cover a poor, black inner-city area.

On the other hand, many participants argued that precisely *because* of his or her skin color, and the experiences it has forced upon him or her, a black reporter would have a greater interest in and bring a better understanding to covering black concerns than a white reporter would. Lyle observed that "the circumstances imposed upon them have forced Negroes, and particularly ghetto dwellers, into distinct social patterns." Thus, in some cases, reporters must try to interpret one culture for another, Lyle said, and so experts are needed.[21]

Conference participants offered several ingenious suggestions for bringing this needed expertise into the media. Besides the obvious method of hiring minority reporters, participants suggested, at the Washington symposium, that the media hire reporter aides—people from the black community who would not serve as full-time staffers but who would be paid for assisting reporters who did not know their way around the black community.

At the same conference, the director of the Seattle Model Cities program suggested that the media should involve all levels of the community, especially the black community, in an advisory role. He said that each medium should set up a citizens' advisory board which could provide the medium with feedback about its performance.[22]

At the Maryland lecture series, Heisler said that in its efforts to cover better the inner city, the *Baltimore Evening Sun*, in addition to appointing and training a staff of urban affairs reporters and hiring more black journalists, recruited writers "from the ranks of volunteer VISTA workers who had worked and studied in the ghetto" and who had intimate knowledge of the inner city.[23]

Participants at the Columbia conference stated that the media should try to find or to train people who are informed about minority groups and suggested that foundations or schools could undertake to train such specialists, who could then be loaned to the media. They noted this would be of particular value in helping smaller newspapers do a more adequate job of interpreting black concerns in depth. In addition, they urged that "editors as well as reporters should seek to sensitize themselves to ghetto needs and to cultivate contacts with ghetto people."[24]

This last observation sounds very similar to one made by Caryl Rivers twelve years after the Columbia conference. It is up to media executives, Rivers said, to seek out representatives of disenfranchised groups and establish sustained contact with them. "Media managers should sit down with such groups on a regular basis to get an idea of what their problems and priorities are," she wrote.[25]

Another method of establishing communications with inner-city residents was discussed by Heisler, who said that over 60 percent of the calls and letters received by an "Action Line"–type of column established by the *Evening Sun* came from inner-city residents. These people have more than their share of frustrating encounters with red tape and brush-offs from bureaucrats, Heisler observed, and they had found both help and a line of communication through the paper's "Direct Line" column.[26]

The vital point in all these suggestions is that reporters and executives need to have or develop a special sensitivity to and understanding of the concerns of minorities. At the Washington symposium, Holman stated, "The color of the skin is not the important thing. The important thing is commitment on the part of the news organization to recognize that there is a lack of communication between the races and that the news organization must help bridge the gap."[27]

IMPROVING COVERAGE

Conference participants offered many proposals to help improve coverage in areas where the media had failed to live up to their own standards of good reporting. Their suggestions were aimed at the encouragement of covering blacks as a normal part of American society and the probing of racial stereotypes; at the exploration of problems facing blacks, particularly local blacks and ghetto dwellers, and the presentation of suggested solutions; and at the coverage of the causes underlying racial conflict. Participants were most concerned that journalists develop resources and training programs to help them become better informed about urban and racial problems.

In 1980, Caryl Rivers made a statement that reiterated a claim frequently made in the 1960s conferences: that media managers simply must do a better job of covering minority communities. "Too often," she said, "the big metro dailies and television stations regard the black and Hispanic communities as alien turf, as remote as the Australian outback." She added that executives are going to have to resist advertising pressures to ignore these areas because they are not where the revenue is. This will not be easy, she said, but it must be done "if American journalism is to do what it's supposed to do: hold a mirror up to society—all of it, not just white, middle-class America."[28]

Participants at the Columbia seminar explored this subject in great detail, calling for coverage of the black community's organizations and its cultural and social events and for "soft" news and human interest stories on black individuals and concerns. They also stated that all black leadership, not only leadership in the civil rights field, should be made visible in the media.

In addition, they called for continuing media attention to the ghetto and for stories that showed the ghetto's communal activities and portrayed ghetto dwellers "as human beings who live, enjoy and suffer like anyone else." They added that the media should encourage ghetto organizations to send in news of their activities, and they suggested that media representatives attend meetings of these groups to explain how the media operate, to teach the groups how to prepare news releases, and to explain what kind of information the media consider newsworthy.[29]

A point stressed at other seminars was the importance of covering black inner-city areas on a regular basis. During the UCLA meeting, Karl Fleming of *Newsweek* said, "[W]e shouldn't wait until the rocks start flying, but [should] go down there every day and cover Watts like you do any beat. Make friends and contacts and finally convince the people that you are an honest man with good personal intent." Jack Jones agreed. He said a reporter has to cover the area regularly and establish relationships with people "who know you and either trust you or at least feel that maybe you are trying to understand."[30] Holman said at the University of Washington symposium that "the reporter, whether he is Black or White, must be given the opportunity to get down into the community often—and not just when there are crises."[31]

Columbia seminar participants suggested teaming a white and a black reporter to work together on ghetto coverage, in hopes that this would make maximum use of their different perspectives and deepen the understanding of each. They added that newspapers should establish special clipping files and other collections of data relevant to minority life so that reporting of minority activities can be presented regularly.[32]

In *Small Voices*, Rivers made the additional point that media executives interested in improving their coverage of minorities must build into the system rewards for reporters who cover these groups. "Reporters do not rush eagerly into dead-end streets," she noted, adding that some journalists motivated by conscience or their own concern will work hard to do good reporting in these areas but will eventually become discouraged if "they keep seeing their stories stuck under the auto body ads on page 32."[33]

Some rewards for minority coverage could be provided through the many reporting competitions held regularly by news organizations and other professional associations. Establishment and promotion of a category for outstanding minority affairs reporting could provide recognition for journalists laboring in those vineyards.

Concerning the problem of coverage that promotes stereotypical images of minorities, British journalist Harold Evans made the most novel suggestion for correcting this situation. He said it is the duty of the press to seek out the truth independently, and this includes exposing the truth about stereotypes. He stated, "If there are popular conceptions about immigrants, for instance, which sway people's minds and government policies, then it is the job of the Press to find out how soundly based these conceptions are." For example, Evans noted that "it was commonly asserted [in Britain] that immigrants batten on the social services," and he indicated that although the British press should have investigated whether or not this idea was true, such effort was left to a national organization, whose examination revealed the stereotype's essential flaws.

Evans is not suggesting that the media should report only information that contradicts a stereotype. He is calling instead for journalists to investigate whether or not a stereotype is based on fact and to report what they find. He notes that the idea of the press initiating such investigations has been criticized by some, but he feels it is necessary because "there is a balance to be redressed." He adds that if the press fails to undertake independent initiatives, untruths will flourish.[34]

Hartmann and Husband make the same point, urging that the British press "adopt a positive attitude toward improving race relations and deliberately seek to publish material which challenges prevailing false stereotypes." They say that when there are widely held misconceptions about blacks, the media "have a responsibility to correct these rather than tacitly supporting them through neglect of contrary information." The authors add that "too often material which has not been consistent with current stereotypes and perspectives has been ignored or buried."[35]

It would seem imperative for journalists to beware of creating new stereotypes, new frameworks on which news about blacks will be fitted. For instance, the coverage studied in this project showed a considerable increase in news about blacks involved in political activities. To some extent, this coverage pattern is simply a reflection of changes in the society. But considering the tenacity of stereotypes in media coverage, it would not be surprising if the media tended to run stories about black politicians whether the stories were of real importance or not, because such stories are familiar and expected, while ignoring stories that do not fit easily into the framework.

Showing the everyday activities of the black community, portraying black Americans as human beings with the same aspirations and frailties as other Americans, and running positive human interest and feature stories about blacks, all are additional methods of combatting stereotypes. Still another is running features tracing the contributions of blacks to American history, music, sports, literature, and other fields; illuminating black history and culture; portraying black American heroes; perhaps even tracing the African influence in black and regional American cuisine, music, dress, and speech. Blacks have a rich history and culture that is largely unknown to white Americans, and the media could help reveal it.

Another step necessary for the media to take in improving their coverage of race relations is conveying to white Americans the problems still facing black citizens. The media need to disabuse themselves and their audiences of the idea that the civil rights revolution solved all the essential problems facing blacks. They need to make clear the many severe obstacles that continue to prevent millions of American blacks from enjoying equality of opportunity in this country: the racism and economic system that trap blacks in low-income jobs and in inner-city ghettos, the substandard schooling that prevents many black children from attaining their intellectual potential, the breakup of family life among many low-income blacks, and the perpetuation of successive generations of black families dependent upon welfare. The situations that frustrate more affluent blacks, like discrimination in promotions and hidden racism, also should be explored.

Referring to the British press, Hartmann and Husband state that the news media "have a positive role to play in attacking racial inequalities and exploitation, and this cannot be achieved without a deliberate attempt to seek out such injustices and expose them." The authors note their study had shown that the media had a vital role in maintaining public awareness of racial injustices and appealing to the public's ideals of equality and fair play.

They cited as an example of positive journalism a British newspaper's campaign against the exploitation of black South African laborers by British firms. The coverage was so extensive and prominently displayed that other media were influenced to take up the story. As a result, the authors say, some of the firms reformed their policies, and the public was informed about matters which they otherwise would not have known—and which they may well have preferred not to know about, the authors observe.[36]

In American journalism, there is still an urgent need for media to once again devote manpower and make a commitment to covering the concerns of their local black communities. The concerns of ghetto residents especially require illumination, because the ghettos are where the forces oppressing black Americans are most concentrated and where the simmering anger of blacks is most likely to explode again into violence. Columbia seminar participants suggested some "bedrock" issues that could be covered in depth, such as lack of available job training for people trapped in the worst-paid jobs, the struggle for community control of schools, and the problems and opportunities of black policemen.[37] Other possible topics include price-gouging in ghetto stores; the paucity of city monies spent for library, health care, recreational, and other facilities in the ghetto; and rapacious landlords.

During the 1960s, Ben Bagdikian raised an important point regarding media coverage of problems. "If American journalism is successful in describing the causes of urban collapse," he said, "it must also suggest remedies or tempt panic." It seems crucial that media coverage of injustices and malfunctions in American society be accompanied by coverage of suggested solutions, or the result may well be to increase a sense of the problems' insolubility and to strengthen the well-intentioned white's sense of impotence to help effect change.

Bagdikian suggested that the media should systematically and regularly collect and publish a wide spectrum of suggested solutions to urban problems. "Newspapers and broadcasters ought to seek out the most authoritative and creative thinkers on urban problems and display their ideas clearly and fairly, keeping them distinct from the paper's own positions." He added that it was appalling to consider how much newsprint since the 1930s had been devoted to the flaws of the welfare system, and how a basic change—except for totally abandoning the system—had almost never been proposed.

Claiming that the media had done little to inform people about the many rational ideas available on how to facilitate racial change, Bagdikian said, "If we are inhibiting both the unpleasant news and the presentation of novel social ideas because we feel people must be protected from the physical and intellectual realities of their lives, then we are in an even more critical condition than our urban riots tell us we are."[38]

Other techniques for presenting possible solutions include running news and feature stories on measures suggested both by experts and by the people most directly affected by the problems, debates about the most effective methods of solving the problems, and reports of successful experiments and projects. Of vital importance, it would seem, is avoiding what the 1960s conference participants criticized as "white people deciding how to solve black people's problems." Perhaps one of the most useful roles the media could serve, in illuminating possible solutions to problems affecting blacks, is providing an avenue through which blacks at all levels of the community could communicate their convictions, born of their own experiences, about what measures are needed to solve these problems.

The need to outline solutions was addressed by Sylvan Meyer in his assessment of the southern press's performance during the school desegregation crisis. Discussing the newspapers' "sins of omission," Meyer said that high on the list of flunked opportunities was a lack of "what do we do next?" coverage. Most southern papers, he said, avoided clearly defining school desegregation problems and their possible answers. "Papers which might send a reporter to a dozen farflung cities to investigate better garbage collection techniques did not probe for balm for the more crucial racial conflict in their midst." And yet, Meyer noted, "In any conflict possible solutions are bona fide news, and suggesting solutions is legitimate, even demanded, editorial column fare."[39]

Columbia seminar participants agreed that the media should run not only diagnoses of problems but prescriptions for remedies. They felt that background pieces on problems rarely explored concrete remedial measures, which was what the ghetto public wanted to hear about, because opinions varied so widely about what must be done. A solution to this situation might be for the media to include the whole range of proposals for remedies, to educate the public, and to provide a basis for public discussion and debate. Participants also suggested that the media might serve to bridge the communications gap between blacks and whites by reporting ghetto dwellers' ideas about what needed to be done.[40]

They suggested a variety of methods by which journalists could become better informed about the complexities of the problems facing blacks, particularly ghetto dwellers. One idea developed at the seminar was setting up a clearinghouse that journalists could consult for information about inner-city housing and employment needs, the composition and effectiveness of different civil rights organizations, and a host of other topics. They said the media make more use of the extensive data and insights on the ghetto gathered by social scientists and said this kind of material could be more fully utilized in, for instance, assessing the riot potential of a given city or ascertaining the real meaning of black crime statistics.[41]

They urged that journalism schools give students a better understanding of racial and urban problems and of how to cover them, and this idea was echoed by participants at other 1960s conferences and in several discussions of media coverage of minorities published in the 1970s.

At the Chicago seminar, Bagdikian stated that "reporting basic conditions in the ghetto takes a higher level of knowledge and a more careful selection of journalists than exist in many news organizations." He noted that the Kerner Commission had recommended an Institute of Urban Communications be established to inform journalists about the problems of the city. But Bagdikian believed a more productive project would be the institution of courses on this topic in universities that already have competence in urban studies.[42]

Although the Kerner Commission's vision of the institute never became a reality, the Gannett Fund did provide Northwestern University's Medill School of Journalism with a grant that was used to fund a Center for Urban Journalism. Heisler said that when the

Baltimore Evening Sun management realized that it had to provide specialized training "to get the expert reporters we needed to cope with the inner city," it began sending reporters to this center.[43]

Several urban journalism courses have been established in universities across the country, and a few courses on the mass media and minorities have been offered, but these kinds of courses are not widespread. Not much is being done in most journalism schools to train journalists to cover better the inner city and to recognize how racism impacts there, or even to sensitize students to the special problems and challenges of minority coverage.

Another means of improving reporters' ability to cover the city would be for professional journalistic organizations occasionally to hold week-long seminars on urban affairs to which journalists could be sent for in-service training. This kind of seminar is usually held to update journalists in new developments in press law or freedom of information matters; it also could be used to inform reporters about covering the inner city. Also useful would be some kind of national information center and clearinghouse through which reporters could have access to the best works on the city done by social scientists and others.

Another desired coverage improvement often mentioned at the conferences was that the media, when reporting social protests, should dig below the surface of the events to uncover and explain the underlying causes. This change, like others already discussed, would require a rethinking of traditional journalistic practices. News executives would have to direct reporters to go beyond the usual approach of covering social protests as episodes. Instead, journalists would need to go deeper, to portray what Hodding Carter III refers to as "the wave beneath the froth."

Speaking of southern newspapers, but noting that his words applied to American journalism in general, Carter said at the Missouri conference that most southern papers did not cover the root causes of segregation and community problems. He said the papers were good at reporting clean-up drives but failed to examine the causes of the poverty which resulted in over half the community being in run-down condition. They were good at pointing out the number of blacks being trained in local industry but failed to discuss why personnel managers could honestly say, "We would like to hire more, but we can't find them." They were good at reporting that the local school would be desegregated, he said, but bad at pointing out that because of its location, the school would remain predominantly black after integration.

What was urgently needed throughout the media, Carter said, was the kind of reporting "that pays close attention not to the froth that comes up on a deep, deep wave but to the wave itself."[44] This kind of reporting, although requiring more effort than simply treating protests as crime stories, would greatly improve coverage of any kind of protest, racial or otherwise.

Another change that would similarly improve protest coverage would be for media executives to cease directing reporters to emphasize the most sensational and violent aspects of the events. It is not suggested that violence be played down or ignored but that it instead be reported in perspective.

During the 1960s conferences various participants mentioned how important it was for reporters covering protests and conflicts not to rely on official sources for their information and not to become mouthpieces for police or government officials. The participants explained that the reporters' identification with the police contributed to black distrust of the media. In addition, if only the official side is presented, readers are exposed to only the viewpoint of those concerned with preserving the status quo.

If members of the press do not talk to the protesters and seek to understand and present clearly their grievances, the protesters' perspective will not be made available to the public. The probable result will be that readers will become fearful and hostile toward the protesters and their cause without ever really understanding them.

Reporters could do a better job of presenting the protesters' concerns if they had already developed sources in the black community and had acquired an understanding of the forces operating there. Adequate coverage of the protesters' cause might well require follow-up stories in which reporters could use their already established contacts and knowledge. Columbia conference participants also suggested that to enable reporters to provide adequate coverage of pre-riot or post-riot perspectives on causes or programs, the media should organize a quick-reference file of relevant materials, similar to the ready obituary file most media maintain on prominent persons.[45]

INVOLVING BLACK AMERICANS

One of the suggestions most often urged since the 1960s was that the media take the initiative to open channels of communication with the black community. Several such efforts were undertaken in cities across the country, one of the most interesting being a nineteen-month experiment in Seattle. A communications council of media executives and representatives of the black community was organized in that city in 1968.

The seven media members of the council included the managing editors of the city's two newspapers, the four area television station managers, and the general manger of a soul radio station, while the seven black members included a minister, a judge, the directors of the local Urban League and Model Cities Program, and a member each from the local chapters of the Black Student Union, the Student Nonviolent Coordinating Committee, and the Black Panther Party.

The council's input was not limited to these fourteen people, however. Reporters, other media personnel, and members of the black community were frequent guests at the council's meetings, either by invitation or at their own request. A total of 124 persons (64 white and 60 black) attended at least one of the council's fourteen meetings held between June of 1968 and the end of 1969. The meetings were discontinued when the council's funding was exhausted and Lawrence Schneider, who served as moderator, was similarly exhausted, he reported.[46]

Schneider said the council's purpose was to inform the council's media members of the black community's concerns and to provide a clear and continuous channel through which the black community could communicate with media decision makers. The council's meetings were not reported, because a guarantee of anonymity was required to insure complete freedom of expression.

The council's meetings were sometimes heated and always educational, and through them all, Schneider wrote, one could hear "black men tell of the pain of being black, of being an invisible, powerless minority in a white society which for generations had ignored or abused them."[47]

The council did indeed become a useful channel of communication, Schneider reported. Among media members, it led to a growing recognition of black perceptions of white society and a gradual willingness to use their media to help bridge the gap between the two societies. It also enabled young and older black persons with widely divergent views on the desirability of integration versus separation to meet in a noncombative situation where they eventually were able to communicate with each other and develop respect for each other. Finally, it established some mutually useful contacts between members of the press and young black militants.[48]

The communication that occurred at the council also affected the media's coverage, Schneider reported. Coverage of black concerns increased during the life of the council, and stories and television programs appeared which had been influenced by council discussion. Both newspapers opened their pages to the reporting of black affairs, from more hard-news stories and pieces on blacks expressing their frustrations to articles on black fashions and foods and material on black history, experiences, and attitudes.

Schneider noted that media executives, although they were accustomed to setting policy, were not accustomed to attempting to affect the racial attitudes of their staffs. "Such attitudes," Schneider observed, "are more likely to be affected through contact with members of other races than they are through memorandums from corporate executives."[49] Yet to some extent the executives' participation in the council did have some effect upon their employees. As one executive said, his involvement with the council made both his superiors and his employees more aware of racial problems and had impressed them with the knowledge that he considered the quality of racial reporting important. He said the increased understanding the council meetings gave him had affected his assignment of employees to various areas of racial coverage.[50]

Despite all these benefits, and the participants' own keen sense of the council's value, Schneider said the council was not a success, in the sense that it did not also fulfill his original hope that it would achieve a sense of community in Seattle. As a result of the council, "Individuals are more aware," Schneider wrote, "but that awareness has not yet translated itself into media reporting which has succeeded in creating a community of people who are pleased with one another's company."[51]

By any less stringent standards, however, the council's achievements look impressive. Not only did the members begin to bridge a communications and credibility gap between the media and blacks, but representatives of varying segments of the black community and nonparticipating personnel in the white media were affected and coverage was increased, was more accurate and perceptive, and was approached in innovative ways.

Schneider wrote that although the council did not completely solve race-reporting problems in Seattle, it did demonstrate that such a council could be "a valuable instrument for those who care about working to solve today's racial problems."[52] The Seattle council appears to have been a most effective medium for establishing communications and improving the quality of coverage. Its achievements might well serve as encouragement and as a model for persons interested in making a similar effort.

FINDING MINORITY JOURNALISTS

The necessity of bringing more minority reporters into journalism has been urged constantly since the 1960s and was perhaps most strongly expressed by the Kerner Commission. Stating that the journalistic profession had been "shockingly backward" in recruiting, hiring, training, and promoting blacks, the commission said, "It is unacceptable that the press, itself the special beneficiary of fundamental constitutional protections, should lag so far behind other fields in giving effect to the fundamental human right to equality of opportunity."[53]

Yet this goal is by no means easy to achieve. As numerous sources have noted, many blacks have a deep distrust of the white media, because they see it presenting a distorted picture of the world and serving the interests of the white power structure. Because they had little desire to join the ranks of those who, they feel, have helped oppress blacks, and since the ranks of the white media had long been closed to them, black students traditionally have not considered journalism a viable career option. Many of those who entered the white media during the past two decades, minority journalists say, have become disillusioned at the racism still present in the media and the lack of opportunity for advancement.

Today, educators who train minority journalists state they have difficulty placing their graduates and note the unemployment rate among black journalism graduates is twice as high as that of white ones. Part of this problem stems from factors already discussed—erosion of media executives' commitment to hiring minorities, editors' fear that minority journalists will not be readily accepted and their distrust of minority perspectives, and competition between minority journalists and women in an already crowded job market. But the media's need to hire minority journalists remains imperative, even if it is not as obvious as it was in 1968. One reason for this urgency is an ethical one—the need for integration of the nation's newsrooms, especially the two-thirds of the country's newspapers that have no minority employees. Another is the need for the special knowledge of minority life and concern about minority coverage that minority reporters can bring to the media. Still another is the additional perspective on the reality of American society that minority journalists can offer.

Perhaps most important of all are the skills and insight these journalists can provide, not as representatives of minority groups but as individuals. These abilities have already resulted in coverage improvements and Pulitzer Prizes and other awards for minority journalists and the media that employ them.

Journalists who have analyzed problems involved in the media's hiring of minorities seem to agree that recruitment and training are the keys to ensuring satisfaction. Editors who want to employ capable minority journalists cannot just sit back and wait for candidates to apply; they must go out and seek them, journalists say.

This means they should support efforts to encourage minority high school and college students to consider and train for careers in journalism; they should establish contact with journalism programs at institutions that educate minority students, such as Howard University, Atlanta's Clark College, Florida A&M University, and the Institute for Journalism Education. They should contact the ASNE's minority affairs officer, who strives to keep a current listing of graduating minority journalism students. They could recruit student journalists at annual conferences held at Howard, Hofstra, and other universities, and they might keep track of minority journalists at other news organizations whom they might wish to hire if a position opens up.[54]

In addition, journalists say, news organizations need to establish vigorous affirmative action programs. One of the best minority em-

ployment records in the news business is held by the Gannett newspaper chain, which has a strong commitment to affirmative action at
the corporate level, has worked out minority hiring timetables with
editors and publishers of its individual newspapers, and provides
bonuses for publishers who meet management objectives. The
Knight-Ridder chain also has a management-by-objective program
in which publishers and editors are judged partly on their minority
hiring record, Kotz reports.[55]

One journalist suggests that every newspaper should have minority employment resources. At smaller papers this might be simply a
file of contacts and sources of minority applicants, he says, but
larger papers should have a person who is accountable for hiring
minorities. He suggests that newspapers might have to produce their
own minority staffers through providing internships and sponsoring
students in other training programs.[56]

This is a practice followed by the Gannett chain, which helps
underwrite the cost of summer internship programs at its papers,
while the Gannett Foundation contributes to the training and placement of minority journalists. Knight-Ridder runs a minority internship program and helps defray the costs of hiring and training
minority journalists.[57] Smaller newspapers could establish their
own minority training programs.

Problems in failures to promote minority journalists are another
matter, but one that is not impossible to solve. Kotz writes that the
conflict between black journalists and white editors who do not fully
trust them or their viewpoints "has been immeasureably reduced
when editors have accepted the perspective of minority journalists,
not as intrusions of alien values, but as strengths that can enhance a
newspaper's coverage."[58] These perspectives could greatly enrich a
paper's portrayal of reality for its readers, as could implementation
of the other suggestions presented in this chapter.

NOTES

1. Rivers, pp. 59–61.
2. *Conference on Mass Media and Race Relations*, p. 24.
3. Rivers, p. 56.
4. Schneider, *The Newsman and the Race Story*, pp. 6–7.
5. Ibid., p. 1.

6. *Conference on Mass Media and Race Relations*, p. 24.
7. Schneider, *The Newsman and the Race Story*, p. 5.
8. Ibid., pp. 6–7.
9. Evans, p. 51; emphasis original.
10. Meyer, "The Press and the Schools," p. 44.
11. Evans, p. 51.
12. Young, p. 39; emphasis original.
13. *National Advisory Commission*, pp. 364–66.
14. Schneider, *The Newsman and the Race Story*, pp. 12, 26.
15. Philip S. Heisler, "How Does a Metropolitan Daily Newspaper Cover the Inner City?" in Midura, *Why Aren't We Getting Through?* p. 38.
16. Bagdikian, pp. 21–22.
17. *Conference on Mass Media and Race Relations*, p. 16.
18. Rivers, p. 61.
19. Lyle, "Introduction," pp. xii–xiii.
20. "Discussion," in *The Black American and the Press*, pp. 78–79.
21. Lyle, "Epilogue," in *The Black American and the Press*, p. 82.
22. Schneider, *The Newsman and the Race Story*, pp. 12–14.
23. Heisler, p. 37.
24. *Conference on Mass Media and Race Relations*, pp. 14, 19.
25. Rivers, p. 60.
26. Heisler, pp. 40–41.
27. Schneider, *The Newsman and the Race Story*, p. 11.
28. Rivers, p. 61.
29. *Conference on Mass Media and Race Relations*, p. 11.
30. "Discussion," in *The Black American and the Press*, pp. 43–44.
31. Schneider, *The Newsman and the Race Story*, p. 11.
32. *Conference on Mass Media and Race Relations*, p. 18.
33. Rivers, p. 60.
34. Evans, pp. 52–53.
35. Hartmann and Husband, p. 211.
36. Ibid.
37. *Conference on Mass Media and Race Relations*, pp. 13–14.
38. Bagdikian, pp. 22–24.
39. Meyer, "The Press and the Schools," p. 38.
40. *Conference on Mass Media and Race Relations*, pp. 13, 24.
41. Ibid., p. 14.
42. Bagdikian, p. 22.
43. Heisler, p. 37.
44. Hodding Carter III, "The Wave Beneath the Froth," in Fisher and Lowenstein, *Race and the News Media*, p. 57.
45. *Conference on Mass Media and Race Relations*, p. 14.

46. Lawrence Schneider, "A Media-Black Council: Seattle's 19-Month Experiment," *Journalism Quarterly* 47, no. 3 (Aug. 1970), 444.

47. Ibid., pp. 445–46.

48. Ibid., pp. 447–49.

49. Ibid., p. 441.

50. Ibid., p. 448.

51. Ibid., pp. 444, 449.

52. Ibid., p. 439.

53. *National Advisory Commission*, pp. 384, 387.

54. Further information on job fairs and hiring minority journalists may be obtained by contacting Carl Morris, minority affairs director, ASNE, P.O. Box 17004, Washington, D.C. 20041; JOB/NET at University of California, Berkeley; APME; Society of Professional Journalists; Dow Jones Newspaper Fund; National Association of Black Journalists, 525 W. Broadway, Louisville, Ky. 40202; National Association of Hispanic Journalists and Asian American Journalists Association, both in Los Angeles; and Native American Press Association at Penn State.

55. Kotz, "Minority Struggle," pp. 29–30.

56. Lee Stinnett, "Minorities in the Newsroom," *ASNE Bulletin*, March 1981, p. 33.

57. Kotz, "Minority Struggle," pp. 29–30.

58. Ibid., p. 28.

CHAPTER 10
Conclusion

Several common themes seem to run through the suggestions discussed in the previous chapter. Besides the necessity for rethinking some traditional journalistic attitudes and practices, and avoiding the kinds of coverage deficiencies examined in the empirical study reported in this book, many of the proposals seem to urge an extra effort on the part of the media. This effort includes developing experts and resources on racial and urban problems, taking the initiative to establish communications with the black community, seeking out and exposing injustices, becoming more sensitive and knowledgeable about black concerns, and bringing more blacks into the media.

It is easy to see how the various suggestions included here would produce the kind of coverage that fulfills the tenets of the social responsibility theory of the press. The coverage would serve the functions of going beyond factual accuracy to provide the public with the realities underlying news events, it would include the perspectives and ideas of more segments of American society, it would accurately portray various groups within society to each other, it would expose injustices and help clarify ways to bring reality closer to society's ideals, and it would give citizens the kinds of information they need to make rational decisions in self-government.

However, it is perhaps asking a great deal to expect the media to make the kinds of extra effort suggested here in the face of the inertia generated by past racism and journalistic traditions, plus the resistance of advertisers and possibly of readers. But despite the forces operating to maintain the status quo in racial coverage, efforts to improve that coverage would serve the enlightened self-interest of both the media and the public.

During the 1968 University of Chicago conference, one participant stated, "The Negro seeks in America what the white man seeks in America and what the Declaration of Independence and the Constitution assure him: freedom and a chance to make it in our society."[1]

Ten years later, television news correspondent Mal Goode expressed the same idea in different words. When individuals ask him what black people want, he said, "I tell them that the answer is simple. Take out a piece of paper and write down all that you want for yourself, your family and your grandchildren, and all you think you want for anyone who is close to you, and sign my name to it, because that's exactly what I want."[2]

But for many black Americans that goal cannot be attained. Although blacks have made significant advances in many fields since the tumultuous years of the 1960s, nearly every achievement is offset by areas in which very little progress has been made. For example:

• In the South, most barriers to blacks' voting and using public facilities have come down, and the "separate but equal" approach to education has been abolished. However, according to the *Wall Street Journal*'s 1980 series on blacks in America, "racial separation remains the dominant fact of Southern life." Stating that the lives of many—perhaps most—southern blacks have not improved very much, the report added, "Blacks still are held firmly at the bottom of the social and economic pyramid."[3]

• The educational achievements of blacks have increased considerably. During the last twenty years the number of blacks attending college has risen by 400 percent. Black high school graduates are as likely as white high school graduates to go on to college. Yet despite this increase in educational attainment and passage of anti-discrimination-in-hiring laws, during a recession, joblessness among black youths continues to rise faster than it does for other groups, and in prosperous times it falls more slowly. Primarily because of racial discrimination, the *Wall Street Journal* reported, the unemployment rate for black college graduates is higher than it is for white high school dropouts.[4]

• The number of black officeholders has increased greatly, tripling in the last ten years. Yet the number of black officials is only 1 percent of the nation's total. Perhaps more important, 75 percent of the black officials hold local-level offices, and those elected to higher office usually represent areas where urban decay is so far advanced that it cannot be reversed. Representative Shirley Chisholm says that Bedford-Stuyvesant, a blighted section of Brooklyn that is part of her district, is typical of the "shells white leaders leave behind when they abandon an area politically to blacks."[5]

- The black middle class, defined as families having incomes above $15,000 a year and a white-collar job, constitutes one-third of the black population; it has more than doubled since 1960. However, two-thirds of white Americans have middle-class status.[6]

- Blacks seem much more visible in American society, and their presence and achievements are accepted. In 1983 alone the first black astronaut was sent into space, a black golfer won a national championship, a black woman was chosen as Miss America, and a black man ran for president of the United States. The *Wall Street Journal* reported that white acceptance of integration and contacts between blacks and whites have steadily increased in the past twenty years. On the other hand, the paper said, separation of the races remains the norm, and the little social and intellectual interaction between races that occurs does so among "a fairly thin layer" of well-educated, financially secure members of both races.[7]

In the inner cities, where 56 percent of the nation's black population lives, the only changes that have occurred since the 1960s have been for the worse, experts say. And yet, according to Caryl Rivers, if the urban ghettos were to explode again today, most journalists and the white public would be just as shocked and as uninformed about conditions there as they were during the 1960s.[8]

In fact, most of the black concerns mentioned above are not presented in the media, except for the rare study undertaken by a major newspaper or chain. The media generally still have not taken up, for example, the whole question of how well or poorly school integration is working in areas where it has been implemented, or how it has been avoided in many part of the country, or the situation of rural blacks in the South, or segregation in housing and its effect on school segregation, or a host of other concerns affecting black Americans.

British journalist Harold Evans suggested a high standard of media responsibility when he said the press must go beyond handling racial news as a series of episodes. "It is not enough to report a demonstration or disorder," he wrote. "The why of the trouble has to be reported and analysed and commented on—and when the trouble has died down we must stay with the story *until the causes have died away too*."[9]

Despite all their improvements in minority coverage and hiring, however, the American media clearly have not stayed with the racial story until the causes have died away. Admittedly, it is asking much to expect them to do so, considering the myriad of other conflicts and situations about which they are expected to keep the public informed. On the other hand, judging from the proliferation of lifestyle sections and leisure-time material appearing in American newspapers these days, the press does not lack the space or the reporters to provide more thorough coverage of the continuing tragic effects of racism in our society.

Once again, we come back to the inescapable fact that what is lacking is a willingness to do so, either because of indifference or fear of losing advertisers or readers. At nearly all of the 1960s conferences, participants noted that even when the media did cover black problems, their reportage lacked a sense of urgency. Ben Bagdikian perhaps said it best when he observed that although papers often try to influence congressional delegations on issues such as protection of local industry and appropriations for local projects, "it is rare to find the same tenacity in pressing for low-income housing, massive job training and job creation, and other large-scale solutions of urban problems."[10]

Yet bringing that kind of dedication to coverage of racial inequalities is part of the media's job. Jack Lyle, in the UCLA conference report, said that the media were going to have to find ways to make the concerns of blacks important as well as understandable to white readers. This will not be easily achieved, Lyle wrote, but,

Such a resolution . . . is essential if the news media are to fulfill their function of surveillance in a manner which will enable the whole American society to react rationally to this aspect of its environment. Only such a resolution provides hope of achieving through the mass media a rational dialogue between white and black Americans which, in turn, can lead to mutual understanding.[11]

Hartmann and Husband suggest that improving their coverage of minorities might be not only the media's job but also in their own best interests. "It seems probable," the authors write, "that if the news media do not attempt to make known to white Britain the personal cost of prejudice to the black British, then black alienation may in the long run breed violence and conflict that is not readily 'manageable.' " Commenting that the media are considered to "set the agenda" for the public's concerns, the authors add, "If they fail to include the possible consequences of racism and discrimination on the agenda then they may ultimately destroy the status quo they seek to protect."[12]

A *Los Angeles Times* journalist made a similar point shortly after the Watts riot, and his words apply to the current situation as well as they did to the circumstances of 1965. "Obduracy, a refusal to recognize that a problem exists . . . simply crystallizes the danger. Another riot can be put down with force—but at what cost to lives and property!" he wrote, noting that it was to the city's economic and humanitarian interests to find answers. He warned, "In the absence of enlightened press leadership, the rabble-rouser may take over. It is a truce now. It could be war."[13]

During the Washington conference, an angry young black man spoke of his impatience for change and how he was unwilling to wait because "my grandmother, my mother and my daddy waited so long. They have nothing." He said, "Either we talk about what the future is going to hold for us, or we're not going to have a future together." Vowing that he was not going to let his children or his sister's or his friends' children grow up the way he had to grow up, he added, "I'm not scared of you. The only thing I'm scared of is that my people won't have all the fire bombs ready when it is time."

Later in the conference, the youth spoke of the need for blacks to have the opportunity to accomplish, to take pride in their accomplishments, and be able to say, "I am a part of America." "Give us a chance," the man urged. He added, "but don't stop me because I have nothing to lose and many Black people in this nation have nothing to lose." He stated, "This is your problem as well as mine. I have a choice. I can burn this place down and get a job helping rebuild it." But apparently this was not the option he desired, and he added, "Let's get this country together now. . . . And let's get a solution that we can both be happy with."[14]

His words illustrate a fact that is often overlooked—that whites also have a stake in improving race relations, and this interest operates at several levels. The most basic one is avoiding renewed racial strife and violence.

The nation cannot afford to continue to ignore the burning sense of grievance and frustration of low-income, inner-city blacks until their rage once again ignites to destroy human lives and whole tracts of our cities. Shortly before he was killed, Dr. Martin Luther King expressed this idea best in words that are as pertinent today as they were in 1968: "We must learn to live together as brothers or we will perish together as fools."

White Americans' stake in the eradication of racial prejudice also involves still another aspect of enlightened self-interest. As many writers have pointed out, racism imprisons the white man and poisons his life just as surely as it does the black man, but in more subtle ways. John Howard Griffin, author of *Black Like Me*, has noted that as long as black Americans are denied the opportunity, because of the color of their skin, to develop their full human potential, no white Americans are truly free either.[15]

Finally, our nation needs to close the gap between American ideals and American reality. Claims that America is "the land of the free" and offers "liberty and justice for all" have a hollow ring not only to millions of black Americans but to all the other nonwhite peoples of the world as well, as long as equality of opportunity and justice are so obviously denied to many Americans.

During the 1960s, a Swiss journalist commented at the UCLA conference that his editors were interested in the racial confrontation then occurring in the United States because it provided a means of achieving a good understanding of American society. "Particularly," he observed, "it demonstrates the self-correcting aspect which, it seems to me, is more outstanding in the American society than in any other." He said the race-related changes then occurring also showed the workings of the American government, "the mechanism by which the self-correction is implemented." The racial situation was important, he said, because it illustrated a weakness of the United States that was heavily exploited by its enemies and also because of the forces working to correct the contradictions "between the American credo and American reality."[16]

Speaking at the same conference was Gunnar Myrdal, the Swedish sociologist and economist whose *An American Dilemma*, a 1944 study of blacks in the United States, was for many years a classic in the field. Myrdal also addressed the subject of ideals and stated that they are not simply abstract concepts but are also important forces that are slowly but inexorably moving America toward providing equality for *all* its citizens. "Ideals are important social facts when they are firmly anchored in the hearts of the people and become fortified in such institutions as the Constitution," Myrdal said, noting that "people are disquieted when they are not living up to their own ideals."[17]

The American media have many opportunities to contribute to the attainment of American ideals by helping create the conditions in which better race relations can occur. They can expose problems and outline suggested solutions. They can try to open channels of communication with their local black communities, and they can interpret black and white societies to each other. They can explode racial stereotypes and highlight black contributions to American society. They can reflect a picture of America as a multiracial society, and they can show the benefits accruing from a mixing of cultures. They can support efforts to employ minority reporters.

Such a program might make many journalists uneasy, striking them as an attempt to go beyond the media's mandate to gather and report the news. At the Columbia conference, some members of the press became impatient with criticisms that the media had failed to serve as an educational force in the current racial crisis. They said the job of journalists was "to cover the news—not make it." They went on to add that the media should leave the job of uplift to churches, lobbyists, and other groups.[18]

This position may at first sound logical, but as the examples presented in this book have pointed up time and time again, the media cannot escape having an effect on race relations, whether they desire such a role or not. The way they report race-related matters, and also what they fail to report, strongly affect the public's view of the nation's racial situation and contribute to the development of positive or negative attitudes toward members of another race.

Since the media are, by the very nature of their work, thrust into a central role in race relations, it seems only logical that they would strive to perform their jobs in such a way as to contribute toward the development of a healthier and more democratic society, rather than produce coverage that creates even more divisiveness and interracial hostility. The media enjoy a favored position and wield enormous power in American society; surely it would be sensible for them to cover racial matters in a manner that ultimately strengthens that society.

Ralph McGill wrote that when Atlanta's buses and other public facilities were desegregated, one of his greatest satisfactions was to know he had been "one of the many who worked long and patiently at the arduous job of seeing to it that the people of Atlanta knew the facts [about segregation] and the alternatives."[19] If the United States is indeed drifting even further toward racially separate and unequal societies, as the Kerner Commission stated, it seems that one of the most worthwhile tasks a newspaper could undertake would be insuring that its readers know the facts about this growing division and the alternatives to it.

NOTES

1. Hamilton, p. 50.

2. "Black Reporters Urged to Crack Top Ranks," *Editor & Publisher*, 16 Sept. 1978, p. 10.

3. Neil Maxwell, "Minority Report: In Much of the South, Separation of the Races Still Is Key Fact of Life," *Wall Street Journal*, 17 Nov. 1980, p. 1, col. 1.

4. Stevens, "Integration Is Elusive Despite Recent Gains," p. 23, col. 1; Carol Sutton, "How Does the Press Handle the Concerns of Black Americans?" *ASNE Bulletin*, April 1981, p. 33; Charles W. Stevens, Paul Goldberg, Cindy Ris, Keith Harriston, and Carrie Dolan, "Minority Report: Joblessness Worsens Among Black Youths, with No Solution Seen," *Wall Street Journal*, 8 Sept. 1980, p. 1, col. 1.

5. David J. Blum, "Minority Report: Black Politicians Fear They Can't Do Much to Help Their People," *Wall Street Journal*, 29 Oct. 1980, p. 1, col. 1.

6. Ronald Alsop, "Minority Report: Middle-Class Blacks Worry About Slipping, Still Face Racial Bias," *Wall Street Journal*, 3 Nov. 1980, p. 1, col. 1.

7. Stevens, "Integration Is Elusive Despite Recent Gains," p. 1.

8. Rivers, pp. 51–52.

9. Evans, p. 51, emphasis added.

10. Bagdikian, p. 23.

11. Lyle, "Epilogue," p. 83.

12. Hartmann and Husband, p. 212.

13. Bassett, p. 43.

14. Schneider, *The Newsman and the Race Story*, pp. 29–30.

15. John Howard Griffin, "Racist Sins of Christians," in Daniel, *The John Howard Griffin Reader* (Boston: Houghton Mifflin, 1968), pp. 437–39.

16. Werner Imhoof, "Comment by Werner Imhoof," in Lyle, *The Black American and the Press*, p. 57.

17. Myrdal, p. 8.

18. *Conference on Mass Media and Race Relations*, p. 23.

19. McGill, p. 297.

Appendix A

Percentage of Blacks in Populations of Four Cities in 1950, 1960, 1970, 1980

City	Year			
	1950	1960	1970	1980
New York	10%	14%	21%	25%
Atlanta	37%	38%	51%	67%
Boston	5%	9%	16%	32%
Chicago	14%	23%	33%	40%

NOTE: Figures for 1950 through 1970 from U.S. Dept. of Commerce, Bureau of the Census, and U.S Dept. of Labor, Bureau of Labor Statistics, The Social and Economic Status of Negroes in the United States, 1970 (Washington, D.C.: Government Printing Office, 1971). Figures for 1980 from U.S. Dept. of Commerce, Bureau of the Census, 1980 Census of Population and Housing, Final Population and Housing Unit Count (Washington, D.C.: Government Printing Office, 1981), and 1980 Census of Population, vol. 1, Characteristics of the Population, ch. C, General Social and Economic Characteristics, pt. 23, Massachusetts (Washington, D.C.: Government Printing Office, 1983).

Appendix B

Estimated Percentage of News Hole Devoted to Coverage of Blacks in Four Newspapers During Three Time Periods

Newspaper	Time Period		
	1950s	1960s	1970s
NYT	.0050	.0254	.0190
AC	.0116	.0404	.0354
BG	.0020	.0280	.0319
CT	.0084	.0258	.0271

NOTE: Total available news space estimated on the basis of annual reports of each newspaper's ratio of advertising to news content as published in "Quantitative Analysis of the Content of Morning, Evening and Sunday Newspapers for the Year 1958," Editor & Publisher, 21 March 1959, pp. 66, 68-70, and "Ad—News Ratio for 238 Dailies in 83 Markets," Editor & Publisher, 14 April 1979, pp. 12-13, 54.

Appendix C

Topics Covered in Stories About Black Problems

Time Period	Newspaper	Problems
1950s	NYT	Housing discrimination in Washington, D.C.
1960s	NYT	Harlem dwellers' hardships during local transit strike. Why blacks can't own businesses in Harlem. Starving poor in Mississippi.
	AC	Local justice to poor not equal. Environmental problems in local ghetto. County work camps in Georgia. Poverty, unemployment.
	BG	Local poverty, welfare. City's failure to provide lunches in ghetto schools. Why blacks remain in ghetto when could afford to move out. Failure of southern law to prosecute whites who harm blacks.
1970s	NYT	Crime in local ghetto. Local housing discrimination. Inflation erodes black income gains. Black employment picture remains bleak. Problems of black professional persons. Problems of children of the poor. Southern discrimination against voter registrants. Misconceptions about welfare recipients. Displacement of blacks by urban renewal. Crime in black ghettos in St. Louis. Lack of progress in law enforcement.
	AC	Hunger among local blacks. Health problems of poor in Georgia.

continued

Appendix C (*Continued*)

Time Period	Newspaper	Problems
		Low life expectancy in South Carolina.
		Rise of cancer among blacks.
		Health problems.
		Census flaws affect welfare programs.
		Unemployment among black youths.
		Blacks remain at bottom of economic ladder.
		Problems of black professional women.
		Crime in black ghettos in St. Louis.
		Fear between blacks and whites.
		Increase of white hate groups.
	BG	Hostility in local schools.
		Rise of cancer among blacks.
		Cause of blacks has been abandoned nationally.
		Black wages still lag behind those of whites.
	CT	Failure of federal grants for juvenile offenders to help poor and minority youngsters.
		Discrimination against blacks in criminal justice system.
		Inadequacy of library services in city's black neighborhoods.
		Effects of recession on affirmative action programs.
		Hostility between blacks and whites in Detroit.
		Rise of cancer among blacks.
		Health problems.
		Inferior health care available to blacks.

Bibliography

BOOKS

Belfrage, Sally. *Freedom Summer*. New York: Viking Press, 1965.

Budd, Richard W., Robert K. Thorp, and Lewis Donohew. *Content Analysis of Communications*. New York: Macmillan, 1967.

Conference on Mass Media and Race Relations. Conducted for the Community Relations Service of the U.S. Department of Justice by the American Jewish Committee. New York: American Jewish Committee, 1968.

Daly, Charles U., ed. *The Media and the Cities*. Chicago: Univ. of Chicago Center for Policy Study, 1968.

Daniel, Bradford, ed. *The John Howard Griffin Reader*. Boston: Houghton Mifflin, 1968.

Farmer, James. *Lay Bare the Heart: An Autobiography of the Civil Rights Movement*. New York: Arbor House, 1985.

Fisher, Paul L., and Ralph L. Lowenstein, eds. *Race and the News Media*. Proceedings of a conference sponsored by Anti-Defamation League of B'nai B'rith and Freedom of Information Center, Univ. of Missouri, 14–18 Nov. 1965. New York: Praeger, 1967.

Gannett News Service, special report. *Equality: America's Unfinished Business*. Articles reprinted from Gannett Newspapers. Fort Myers, Fla.: News Press, 1981.

Good, Paul. *The Trouble I've Seen: White Journalist/Black Movement*. Washington, D.C.: Howard Univ. Press, 1975.

Graham, Hugh Davis. *Crisis in Print: Desegregation and the Press in Tennessee*. Nashville: Vanderbilt Univ. Press, 1967.

Harrison, John M., and Harry H. Stein, eds. *Muckraking Past, Present and Future*. University Park: Pennsylvania State Univ. Press, 1973.

Harriss, Julian, Kelly Leiter, and Stanley Johnson. *The Complete Reporter: Fundamentals of News Gathering, Writing, and Editing*. 3rd ed. New York: Macmillan, 1977.

Hartmann, Paul, and Charles Husband. *Racism and the Mass Media: A Study of the Role of the Mass Media in the Formation of White Beliefs and Attitudes in Britain.* Totowa, N.J.: Rowman & Littlefield, 1974.

Hernton, Calvin C. *Sex and Racism in America.* New York: Grove Press, 1966.

Leigh, Robert D., ed. Commission on Freedom of the Press. *A Free and Responsible Press, A General Report on Mass Communication: Newspapers, Radio, Motion Pictures, Magazines and Books.* Chicago: Univ. of Chicago Press, 1947.

Lewis, Anthony, and the New York Times. *Portrait of a Decade: The Second American Revolution.* New York: Random House, 1964.

Lyle, Jack, ed. *The Black American and the Press.* Proceedings of a conference of UCLA Foreign Journalism Awards Program, 1967. Los Angeles: Ward Ritchie, 1968.

McCombs, Maxwell, Donald Lewis Shaw, and David Grey. *Handbook of Reporting Methods.* Boston: Houghton Mifflin, 1976.

McGill, Ralph. *The South and the Southerner.* Boston: Little, Brown, 1963.

Mars, Florence. *Witness in Philadelphia.* Baton Rouge: Louisiana State Univ. Press, 1977.

Marzolf, Marion, and Melba Tolliver. *Kerner Plus 10: Minorities and the Media: A Conference Report.* Sponsored by the Howard R. Marsh Center for the Study of Journalistic Performance, 22 April 1977. Ann Arbor: Univ. of Michigan Press, 1977.

Merrill, John Calhoun. *The Imperative of Freedom: A Philosophy of Journalistic Autonomy.* New York: Hastings House, 1974.

Merrill, John C., and Ralph D. Barney, eds. *Ethics and the Press: Readings in Mass Media Morality.* New York: Hastings House, 1978.

Meyer, Philip. *Return to 12th Street: A Follow-up Survey of Attitudes of Detroit Negroes, October, 1968.* Detroit: Detroit Free Press, 1968.

Midura, Edmund M., ed. *Why Aren't We Getting Through? The Urban Communication Crisis.* Later reprinted as *Blacks and Whites: The Urban Communication Crisis.* Washington, D.C.: Acropolis Books, 1971.

Race and the Press. London: Runnymede Trust, 1971.

Report of the National Advisory Commission on Civil Disorders. New York: New York Times Co., 1968.

Rubin, Bernard, ed. *Small Voices and Great Trumpets: Minorities and the Media.* New York: Praeger, 1980.

Schneider, Lawrence. *The Newsman and the Race Story.* Report of a symposium for newsmen of Washington and Oregon, 28–29 June 1968. Seattle: Univ. of Washington School of Communications, 1968.

Siebert, Fred S., Theodore Peterson, and Wilbur Schramm. *Four Theories of the Press: The Authoritarian, Libertarian, Social Responsibility and Soviet Communist Concepts of What the Press Should Be and Do.* Urbana: Univ. of Illinois Press, 1956.

Simpson, George E. *The Negro in the Philadelphia Press.* Philadelphia: Univ. of Pennsylvania Press, 1936.

Sloan, Irving J., ed., *The Blacks in America, 1492–1977: A Chronology and Fact Book.* 4th ed. Dobbs Ferry, N.Y.: Oceana Publications, 1977.

Spearman, Walter, and Sylvan Meyer. *Racial Crisis and the Press.* Atlanta: Southern Regional Council, 1960.

U.S. Department of Commerce. Bureau of the Census. *1980 Census of Population and Housing, Final Population and Housing Unit Count.* Washington, D.C.: Government Printing Office, 1981.

————. *1980 Census of Population,* vol. 1, ch. C, pt. 23. Washington, D.C.: Government Printing Office, 1983.

U.S. Department of Commerce, Bureau of the Census, and U.S. Department of Labor, Bureau of Labor Statistics. *The Social and Economic Status of Negroes in the United States, 1970.* Washington, D.C.: Government Printing Office, 1971.

Weber, Ronald, ed. *The Reporter as Artist: A Look at the New Journalism Controversy.* New York: Hastings House, 1974.

Women Studies Program and Policy Center, George Washington University. *A Newspaper Study: New Directions for News.* Washington, D.C.: George Washington Univ., 1983.

ARTICLES

"Ad-News Ratio for 238 Dailies in 83 Markets." *Editor & Publisher,* 14 April 1979, p. 12, 13, 54.

Alexander, Charles P. "Bad Tidings for the Jobless." *Time,* 13 Dec. 1982, pp. 54–55.

Alsop, Ronald. "Minority Report: Middle-Class Blacks Worry About Slipping, Still Face Racial Bias." *Wall Street Journal,* 3 Nov. 1980, p. 1, col. 1.

ASNE Committee on Minority Employment, Committee on Education in Journalism. "ASNE on Minorities." *Columbia Journalism Review,* 11, no. 1 (May/June 1972), 51.

Bagdikian, Ben H. "Editorial Responsibility in Times of Urban Disorder." In Daly, ed. *The Media and the Cities.* Chicago: Univ. of Chicago Center for Policy Study, 1968, pp. 13–24.

Bassett, James. "Watts and the Need for Press Involvement." In Fisher and Lowenstein, eds. *Race and the News Media.* New York: Praeger, 1967, pp. 37–43.

Bender, Michelle. "The Black Community—Whitewashed in the News? Can Coverage Be Improved?" *American Press,* May 1968, pp. 30–31, 58.

Bennett, Lerone, Jr. "The White Media." In Daly, ed. *The Media and the Cities*. Chicago: Univ. of Chicago Center for Policy Study, 1968, pp. 7–12.

"Black Reporters Urged to Crack Top Ranks." *Editor & Publisher*, 16 Sept. 1978, pp. 10–11.

Blanchard, Eric D. "The Poor People and the 'White Press.'" *Columbia Journalism Review* 7, no. 3 (Fall 1968), 61–65.

Blum, David J. "Minority Report: Black Politicians Fear They Can't Do Much to Help Their People." *Wall Street Journal*, 29 Oct. 1980, p. 1, col. 1.

Boskin, Joseph. "Denials: The Media View of Dark Skins and the City." In Rubin, ed. *Small Voices and Great Trumpets: Minorities and the Media*. New York: Praeger, 1980, pp. 141–47.

Breed, Warren. "Social Control in the Newsroom: A Functional Analysis." *Social Forces* 33, no. 4 (May 1955), pp. 326–35.

Brown, Claude. "The Ghetto View of Crime." *Race Relations Reporter*, Nov. 1974, pp. 16–18.

Bruce, Beverlee. "Comment by Beverlee Bruce." In Lyle, ed. *The Black American and the Press*. Los Angeles: Ward Ritchie, 1968, pp. 70–74.

Carter, Hodding III. "Comment by Hodding Carter III." In Lyle, ed. *The Black American and the Press*. Los Angeles: Ward Ritchie, 1968, pp. 38–41.

———. "The Wave Beneath the Froth." In Fisher and Lowenstein, eds. *Race and the News Media*. New York: Praeger, 1967, pp. 54–57.

Carter, Roy E. "Segregation and the News: A Regional Content Study." *Journalism Quarterly* 34, no. 1 (Winter 1957), 3–18.

Chaudhary, Anju G. "Press Portrayal of Black Officials." *Journalism Quarterly* 57, no. 4 (Winter 1980), 636–46.

Consoli, John. "Why Blacks Distrust the Press." *Editor & Publisher*, 28 April 1979, p. 87.

Cox, Clinton. "Meanwhile in Bedford Stuyvesant . . ." *MORE*, Aug. 1976, pp. 18–21.

Dalsimer, Samuel. "The Justice of Persuasion." In Fisher and Lowenstein, eds. *Race and the News Media*. New York: Praeger, 1967, pp. 113–120.

DeMott, John. "White Racism in the Newspaper." *The Masthead* 33, no. 4 (Winter 1981), 6–11.

Diamond, Edwin. "The Agony of Responsibility." *Columbia Journalism Review* 13, no. 5 (Jan./Feb. 1975), 9–15.

———. "Covering the Revolution." In Daly, ed. *The Media and the Cities*. Chicago: Univ. of Chicago Center for Policy Study, 1968, pp. 25–32.

———. "School Busing: A Story in Two Acts." *Columbia Journalism Review* 14, no. 6 (March/April 1976), 35–37.

Douglas, Pamela. "The War on Black Children." *Black Enterprise*, May 1981, pp. 22–27.

Evans, Harold. "A Positive Policy." In *Race and the Press*. London: Runnymede Trust, 1971, pp. 42–53.

Fanning, Lawrence S. "The Media: Observer or Participant?" In Fisher and Lowenstein, eds. *Race and the News Media*. New York: Praeger, 1967, pp. 107–112.

Fedler, Fred. "The Media and Minority Groups: A Study of Adequacy of Access." *Journalism Quarterly* 50, no. 1 (Spring 1973), 109–17.

Fisher, Paul L., and Ralph L. Lowenstein. "Introduction and Guidelines." In Fisher and Lowenstein, eds. *Race and the News Media*. New York: Praeger, 1967, pp. 3–10.

Gieber, Walter. "Two Communicators of the News: A Study of the Role of Sources and Reporters." *Social Forces* 39, no. 1 (Oct. 1960), 76–83.

Gilbert, Ben W. "An Extraordinary Indictment of the Press." *ASNE Bulletin*, April 1968, pp. 13–14.

————. "Race Coverage." *ASNE Bulletin*, Jan. 1968, pp. 1–2, 13.

Gilliam, Dorothy. "What Do Black Journalists Want?" *Columbia Journalism Review* 11, no. 1 (May/June 1972), 48–52.

Gist, Noel P. "The Negro in the Daily Press." *Social Forces* 10, no. 3 (March 1932), 405–11.

Griffin, John Howard. "Racist Sins of Chirstians." In Daniel, ed. *The John Howard Griffin Reader*. Boston: Houghton Mifflin, 1968, pp. 430–442.

Gutierrez, Felix, and Clint C. Wilson II. "The Demographic Dilemma." *Columbia Journalism Review* 17, no. 5 (Jan./Feb. 1979), 53–55.

Hamilton, John A. "Telling It Like It Is." In Daly, ed. *The Media and the Cities*, Chicago: Univ. of Chicago Center for Policy Study, 1968, pp. 45–54.

Hayden, Martin S. "A View from Detroit." In Daly, ed. *The Media and the Cities*. Chicago: Univ. of Chicago Center for Policy Study, 1968, pp. 55–64.

Heisler, Philip S. "How Does a Metropolitan Daily Newspaper Cover the Inner City?" In Midura, ed. *Why Aren't We Getting Through? The Urban Communication Crisis*. Washington, D.C.: Acropolis Books, 1971, pp. 29–42.

Henry, William H., III. "Double Jeopardy in the Newsroom." *Time*, 29 Nov. 1982, p. 90.

Holman, Benjamin F. "How Can the Federal Government Facilitate Communication Within the City?" In Midura, ed. *Why Aren't We Getting Through? The Urban Communication Crisis*. Washington, D.C.: Acropolis Books, 1971, pp. 99–112.

Horn, Vivian, and Mary Young. "The News These Days from Carthage,

Mississippi." *Columbia Journalism Review* 13, no. 5 (Jan./Feb. 1975), 16–19.

Hunt, George P. "The Racial Crisis and the News Media: An Overview." In Fisher and Lowenstein, eds. *Race and the News Media*. New York: Praeger, 1967, pp. 11–20.

Imhoof, Werner. "Comment by Werner Imhoof." In Lyle, ed. *The Black American and the Press*. Los Angeles: Ward Ritchie, 1968, pp. 57–59.

Johnson, Paula B., David O. Sears, and John B. McConahay. "Black Invisibility, the Press and the Los Angeles Riot." *American Journal of Sociology* 76, no. 4 (Jan. 1971), 698–721.

Jones, Jack. "Comment by Jack Jones." In Lyle, ed. *The Black American and the Press*. Los Angeles: Ward Ritchie, 1968, pp. 34–38.

———. "Riot Leaves Sense of Helplessness." In *The View from Watts*. Articles reprinted from the Los Angeles *Times* of 10–17 Oct. 1965. Los Angeles: Los Angeles Times, 1965.

Jones, Robert L., and Roy E. Carter, Jr. "Some Procedures for Estimating 'News Hole' in Content Analysis." *Public Opinion Quarterly* 23, no. 3 (Fall 1959), 399–403.

Kirtz, Bill. "Coverage of Minorities and Hiring Improves." *Editor & Publisher*, 1 Dec. 1979, pp. 17, 32.

Klein, Woody. "The New Revolution: A Postscript." In Fisher and Lowenstein, eds. *Race and the News Media*. New York: Praeger, 1967, pp. 141–158.

———. "News Media and Race Relations: A Self-Portrait." *Columbia Journalism Review* 7, no. 3 (Fall 1968), 42–49.

Kotz, Nick. "Keeping Score." *Columbia Journalism Review* 17, no. 6 (March/April 1979), 24.

———. "The Minority Struggle for a Place in the Newsroom." *Columbia Journalism Review* 17, no. 6 (March/April 1979), 23–31.

Latta, Robert L. "A Content Analysis of News of Black Americans as Presented by the Wichita *Eagle* and a Comparison with Empirical Data." *Journalism Abstracts* 9 (1971), 225.

Lyle, Jack. "Introduction." In Lyle, ed. *The Black American and the Press*. Los Angeles: Ward Ritchie, 1968, pp. ix–xviii.

———. "Epilogue." In Lyle, ed. *The Black American and the Press*. Los Angeles: Ward Ritchie, 1968, pp. 82–83.

McWilliams, Carey. "The Continuing Tradition of Reform Journalism." In Harrison and Stein, eds. *Muckraking Past, Present and Future*. University Park: Pennsylvania State Univ. Press, 1973, pp. 118–34.

Massing, Michael. "Blackout in Television." *Columbia Journalism Review* 21, no. 4 (Nov./Dec. 1982), 38–39, 42–44.

Maxwell, Neil. "Minority Report: In Much of the South, Separation of the Races Still Is Key Fact of Life." *Wall Street Journal*, 17 Nov. 1980, p. 1, col. 1.

Mencher, Mel. "Journalism as Seen by Black Reporters and Students." *Journalism Quarterly* 46, no. 3 (Autumn 1969), 499–504, 544.

Meyer, Sylvan. "The Press and the Schools." In Spearman and Meyer, *Racial Crisis and the Press.* Atlanta: Southern Regional Council, 1960, pp. 30–45.

Moreland, Pamela. "Minorities—I: You Editors Make Me Angry." *ASNE Bulletin,* May/June 1982, pp. 6–8.

Myrdal, Gunnar. "The Racial Crisis in Perspective." In Lyle, ed. *The Black American and the Press.* Los Angeles: Ward Ritchie, 1968, pp. 5–15.

————. "Comment by Gunnar Myrdal." In Lyle, ed. *The Black American and the Press.* Los Angeles: Ward Ritchie, 1968, pp. 22–25.

Newfield, Jack. "Is There a 'New Journalism'?" In Weber, ed. *The Reporter as Artist: A Look at the New Journalism Controversy.* New York: Hastings House, 1974, pp. 299–304.

Noland, Thomas. "Old News from the New South." *Columbia Journalism Review* 18, no. 1 (May/June 1979), 41.

Novak, Michael. "Why the Working Man Hates the Media." In Merrill and Barney, eds. *Ethics and the Press: Readings in Mass Media Morality.* New York: Hastings House, 1978, pp. 108–17.

Ott, Thomas. "Hodding Carter Raps Foreign-News Coverage." *Youngstown Vindicator* (Youngstown, Ohio), 18 May 1985, p. 19.

Paletz, David L., and Robert Dunn. "Press Coverage of Civil Disorders: A Case Study of Winston-Salem, 1967." *Public Opinion Quarterly* 33, no. 3 (Fall 1969), 328–45.

Payne, Les. "Black Reporters, White Press—and the Jackson Campaign." *Columbia Journalism Review* 23, no. 2 (July/Aug. 1984), 32–37.

Pinkham, Lawrence. "The Role of Public Television." In Daly, ed. *The Media and the Cities.* Chicago: Univ. of Chicago Center for Policy Study, 1968, pp. 75–86.

Poston, Ted. "The American Negro and Newspaper Myths." In Fisher and Lowenstein, eds. *Race and the News Media.* New York: Praeger, 1967, 63–72.

Pride, Richard A., and Daniel H. Clarke. "Race Relations in TV News: A Content Analysis of the Networks." *Journalism Quarterly* 50, no. 2 (Summer 1973), 319–28.

"Quantitative Analysis of the Content of Morning, Evening, and Sunday Newspapers for the Year 1958." *Editor & Publisher,* 21 March 1959, pp. 66, 68–70.

Rivers, Caryl. "Covering the Disenfranchised: A Working Reporter's Notes." In Rubin, ed. *Small Voices and Great Trumpets: Minorities and the Media.* New York: Praeger, 1980, pp. 46–63.

Roberts, Churchill. "The Presentation of Blacks on Television Network Newscasts." *Journalism Quarterly* 52, no. 1 (Spring 1975), 50–55.

Schneider, Lawrence. "A Media-Black Council: Seattle's 19-Month Experiment." *Journalism Quarterly* 47, no. 3 (Aug. 1970), 439–49.

Sentman, Mary Alice. "Black and White: Disparity in Coverage by Life Magazine from 1937 to 1972." *Journalism Quarterly* 60, no. 3 (Autumn 1983), 501–8.

Shoquist, Joseph W. "The Role of the Press in a Continuing Urban Crisis." In Midura, ed. *Why Aren't We Getting Through? The Urban Communication Crisis.* Washington, D.C.: Acropolis Books, 1971, pp. 43–60.

Stanley, Frank L., Jr. "Race, Poverty and the Press." *ASNE Bulletin*, Sept. 1967, pp. 1–2, 12.

Stein, Harry H., and John M. Harrison. "Muckraking Journalism in Twentieth Century America." In Harrison and Stein, eds. *Muckraking Past, Present and Future.* University Park: Pennsylvania State Univ. Press, 1973, pp. 11–22.

Stempel, Guido, III. "Visibility of Blacks in News and News-Picture Magazines." *Journalism Quarterly* 48, no. 2 (Summer 1971), 337–39.

Stevens, Charles W. "Minority Report: Integration Is Elusive Despite Recent Gains; Social Barriers Remain." *Wall Street Journal*, 29 Sept. 1980, p. 1, col. 1.

Stevens, Charles W., Paul Goldberg, Cindy Ris, Keith Harriston, and Carrie Dolan. "Minority Report: Joblessness Worsens Among Black Youths, with No Solution Seen." *Wall Street Journal*, 8 Sept. 1980, p. 1, col. 1.

Stinnett, Lee. "Minorities in the Newsroom." *ASNE Bulletin*, March 1981, pp. 32–33.

Sutton, Carol. "How Does the Press Handle the Concerns of Black Americans?" *ASNE Bulletin*, April 1981, pp. 32–33.

Tatro, Helen Louise. "Local News Coverage of Blacks in Five Deep South Newspapers, 1950 to 1970." *Journalism Abstracts* 10 (1972), 336.

Weisman, John. "Why TV Is Missing the Picture in Central America." *TV Guide*, 15 Sept. 1984, pp. 2–12.

Wheat, Warren. "It Was a Little Thing, But It Gave Hope." In Gannett News Service. *Equality: America's Unfinished Business.* Fort Myers, Fla.: News Press, 1981, p. 7.

Wicker, Tom. "Introduction." In *Report of the National Advisory Commission on Civil Disorders.* New York: New York Times Co., 1968, pp. v–xi.

Wickham, DeWayne. "For Blacks on Daily Newspapers: The Same Old Song." *Black Enterprise*, Feb. 1979, pp. 44–48.

Wilkins, Roger. "Further More: From Silence to Silence." *MORE*, July 1975, pp. 27, 23.

Williams, Edwin N. "Dimout in Jackson." *Columbia Journalism Review* 9, no. 2 (Summer 1970), 56–58.

Young, Hugo. "The Treatment of Race in the British Press." In *Race and the Press*. London: Runnymede Trust, 1971, pp. 29–41.

UNPUBLISHED MATERIAL

Andrews, Greg. Speech on "Blacks in the Media," at Black History Month program, Youngstown State University, Youngstown, Ohio, 21 Feb. 1983.

Aubespin, Mervin. Speech during viewer call-in program, ASNE annual meeting. Washington, D.C., 12 April 1985.

Beatty-Brown, Florence Rebekah. "The Negro as Portrayed by the St. Louis *Post-Dispatch* from 1920 to 1950." Diss. Univ. of Illinois at Urbana-Champaign, 1951.

Hines, Randall. "Selected Press Coverage of Wounded Knee." Thesis Kent State Univ., 1974.

Kelly, Thomas James. "White Press/Black Man: An Analysis of the Editorial Opinion of the Four Chicago Daily Newspapers Toward the Race Problem, 1954–1968." Ph.D. Diss. Univ. of Illinois at Urbana-Champaign, 1971.

Secrest, Andrew M. "In Black and White: Press Opinion and Race Relations in South Carolina, 1954–1964." Ph.D. Diss. Duke Univ., 1972.

Van Tubergen, Gary Norman. "Racial Attitudes of Gatekeepers." Ph.D. Diss. Univ. of Iowa, 1968.

Index

About the Author

CAROLYN MARTINDALE is Assistant Professor of Journalism at Youngstown State University, Youngstown, Ohio, which has granted her a Distinguished Professor Award. Prior to receiving her M.A. in Journalism she worked as a newspaper reporter and section editor. She has published articles in *Journalism Quarterly*, *College Media Review*, and the *Educational Record*.